FLY FISHING FOR LEADERSHIP

John R Childress
with Christian Bacasa

The best leadership advice I ever got
was from a fly fishing guide.
Both knots and lips should be kept tight.

Cover image by: Adventure_Photo, Getty Images
Book design by: SWATT Books Ltd

First Printing, 2020

ISBN: 978-1-9998918-1-7 (Paperback)
ISBN: 978-1-9998918-2-4 (eBook)

John R Childress
www.johnrchildress.com

FOREWORD

If you are serious about developing as a leader,
then you should take fly fishing to heart!

We asked two highly-regarded leaders, one from the world of finance and venture capital, Lowell Sears, and the other from the fly fishing industry, Jen Ripple, to write a Foreword for this book. They graciously agreed to share their thoughts, each from a different perspective.

LOWELL SEARS

Former Executive, Life Sciences Investor and Avid Fly Angler
Portola Valley, CA

A day on the river or walking the flats, stalking and casting, takes you away mentally and physically from your working world, if you let it. That said, lessons and insights from fly fishing apply to leadership in business and government, as this book richly reveals.

Fly fishing waited to hook me until the 1980s when fellow members of the senior leadership team at Amgen, then a research stage company, introduced me to the sport on a trip to the Big Hole River in Montana.

Amgen subsequently grew into a global pharmaceutical company guided by our leadership. My passion for the art of fly fishing grew at the same time. So, in some ways, it is not surprising for me to link leadership and fly fishing. I should mention that those same Amgen leadership team members are now great friends, and we share fly fishing trips whenever we can.

Over the past 25-plus years as an early stage venture capitalist, helping to fund and build companies and management teams in the life sciences, I often used fly fishing principles to explain decisions or highlight issues. Concepts like pattern recognition, seeing the slight rise in the foam line or the moving opaque forms on the tidal sand, can equate to data matching a clinical trial outcome. Understanding the audience for an investor pitch rolls into matching the hatch and understanding fish behavior. Adapting to changing product demands or capital markets segues into changing fly patterns when the wind, light, or water temperature shifts. I could go on and on.

I have fished in many of the world's great rivers, streams, and oceans, and often bring stories back to the board room. Sometimes for humor, sometimes for emphasis, but mostly I relate those experiences to encourage a discussion about a problem, concern, or opportunity. Fly fishing analogies seem to help people relax. As a result, conversations are more open and forthcoming.

I encourage you to read this book as you would scout a new river for trout or a windy saltwater flat for bonefish. Look for insights and signs that speak to your leadership journey on and off the water. You will find them in this book.

JEN RIPPLE

Editor-in-Chief, Dun Magazine and Avid Fly Angler
Dover, TN

When my son Chip was 8 years old, he skipped third grade and went right into fourth. I was a nervous wreck. I wasn't worried about him academically; that was no problem. But would being the youngest in his class allow him to develop as a leader? I didn't need to worry. He grew up and no matter where in his life he has gone, people have always followed; yes, even in fourth grade. While some like Chip are born with innate leadership potential, others, like me, have to work at it. Regardless of the type of leader you are (or aspire to be), one thing remains the same; when you're a good leader, people will trust and follow you.

We've all fished with "that guy." You know him. He shows up at the launch with $2000 worth of gear, and before you know his name, he's already name-dropped to impress you. He's also fished "all over the world." To the experienced fly angler, it takes less than a minute to realize you're going to spend the next six hours in the drift boat ducking wild casts to avoid a new piercing. But the angler who shows up at the riverbank in well-worn waders, the cork of his rod dirty with fish slime, and offers you a couple of flies that "worked here last time," before quietly walking downstream and leaving you to fish his favorite hole, that's a guy you would gladly follow. If you're wise, it would take you all of five seconds to snip off your fly and take his advice. Good leaders have the same traits as good anglers. You just need to know what they are.

I have to admit that leadership and fly fishing are a correlation I never made before hearing about the concept behind this book. I'm not sure why, because I should have. The connections run as deep and wide as the Missouri River and take as many turns. Each expedition to the water is a unique experience that involves knowledge and planning to be successful. You wouldn't expect to catch wild brook trout on a small mountain stream armed with a 9-weight rod and a bonefish fly any more than you'd expect to be successful in the business world without a deep understanding of your customer. And, just like a good leader chooses the right employees to get the job done, a fly angler knows which fly to choose to match the hatch.

I started fly fishing as an escape from my work, which was all-consuming. What I never expected was that my fly fishing obsession would be my greatest business teacher. If you are serious about improving your leadership skills, then it's time you take fly-fishing to heart. I feel like John and Christian wrote *Fly Fishing for Leadership* at the exact moment in time when it is needed the most. Today's world is marred by confusion, discord, and a lack of good leadership. Maybe the answer to it all will be found in the pages of this book, and in the pursuit of catching fish with a fly.

Photo courtesy of ©John R Childress

A Message From

JOHN R CHILDRESS AND CHRISTIAN BACASA

Fly fishing is not just an extension of the arm, it's an extension of the soul.

A Message from

JOHN R CHILDRESS AND CHRISTIAN BACASA

Nature is the ultimate leader and perhaps that is where the best leadership examples lay.
~Scott Pope

JOHN R CHILDRESS
London, UK

Over the past several decades, the sport of fly fishing has taken on an almost mystical aura. Maybe it began with "The Movie," as my fly fishing friends like to call *A River Runs Through It*. Those hauntingly beautiful scenes of a lone fisherman, waist-deep in the river, casting perfect tight loops through the morning fog enthralled millions. However, long before Hollywood came along, there existed a passionate and somewhat alien group of individuals who chased fish with flies.

So, who are these devoted anglers who fish with flies? And why a book linking fly fishing and leadership?

The avid fly fisher looks (almost) like any other person walking by, sitting in an airplane, or chairing a Board of Directors meeting. But watch their eyes. Those curious, darting, orbs are continually searching for any water flow that may hold a feeding trout or hide a resting migratory salmon. When driving, they slow down while crossing bridges to scan the water, often creating near accidents.

They spend hours staring at a river, a stream, a culvert, a gutter, an irrigation ditch in hopes of seeing a fin break the surface. They even watch the swirls in the toilet bowl, wondering which current would hold the bigger fish.

Yes, they are far from ordinary. Beneath that tanned and windburned exterior lies the heart of a warrior. They are survivors of numerous battles with wily fish, mother nature, shotgun-wielding farmers chasing trespassers, late-night calls from lonely partners, broken down vehicles, and the half-crazed denizens of small-town bars.

They are the campaigners against dams, pipelines, clear-cut logging, and open-pit mines in the last remaining wilderness regions. These are the fathers, mothers, sisters, and brothers who volunteer to teach Scouts, inner-city kids, and our wounded soldiers about the joys of fly fishing, conservation, and life. They often spend as much on environmental causes as they do on beer (well, almost).

And how to tell the hardcore from the occasional angler? Look at the inside of their car, but carefully. It overflows with the flotsam and jetsam of weekend escapes, happy holidays, and dashes to the river after work. At the very minimum, you will unearth several pairs of moldy waders in need of patching. Dozens of spools of fly line, leader, and Tippet material mostly tangled among each other. There will be a minefield of hooks and flies stuck into every crack and piece of fabric. And you can tell the committed (sic) by the assortment of sleeping bags, mattresses that no longer inflate, empty McDonald's cartons, and Snickers wrappers. Plus, at least one empty bottle of Scotch (for medicinal purposes, of course).

Most avid fly anglers have a fishing vehicle dedicated to all things fishing. It's more a mobile fly shop and Star Trek transporter, partially rusted on the outside. There are duplicates and triplicates of everything the fly fisher needs inside, somewhere.

Another characteristic of anglers who fish with flies is their uncanny ability to be talking directly to a person at work or socially, and at the same time be worlds away. They have a rare condition called piscatorial split-brain personality. While being part of a business meeting, they can be reliving a recent event on the river or recalling a mayfly hatch that led to the best fishing of their life. Even reviewing the techniques of tight loop casting, all in that piscine part of their brain. Most people never notice this split attention, except for spouses and loved ones, that is, who long ago gave up trying to capture their full attention.

But get them out on the river with a rod in their hand, and both brains meld together with such laser-like focus that not even a direct lightning strike could distract them from concentrating on a drifting fly or nymph indicator. Their concentration can be so acute they can sense the instant before the fish strikes. While fishing, they are gifted with other-worldly insight, yet at home can't find their car keys and often forget to take out the trash or clean the lint catcher in the dryer.

I must say I am captivated by these creatures. Not only because of the single-minded pursuit that brings them so much joy and satisfaction, but for the qualities they possess and the lessons they learn from fly fishing.

Fly anglers and entrepreneurs are cursed by the same thing: being both excited and frustrated at the same time. ~Scott Wilday

As you will find in this book, the lessons from fly fishing are directly transferable to those in leadership positions who want to become even more effective. When facing challenging issues in the Boardroom or classroom, dealing with difficult people at an Annual General Meeting or on the City Council, integrating two companies after an acquisition, standing for a local or national election, dealing with hormonal teenagers, or rescuing youths from gangs, the lessons learned from fly fishing are invaluable.

This book provides a wealth of examples, stories, and analogies from fly anglers worldwide who have learned, sometimes painfully, essential leadership lessons from fly fishing. You don't have to be one of these crazed and wonderful fly fishers to appreciate and gain value from this book. But you do have to be curious and interested in learning how to be a better leader, a better spouse, a better parent, better CEO, better Congressman, better pastor, or just plain better human being.

To be clear, this is not a book of interviews with celebrities who occasionally fly fish, have the most expensive equipment, and go on exotic fishing trips once or twice a year. I have sought out those who spend as much time fishing as you and I spend at the office. They have experienced the best and the worst of their sport and the people in it. They see both "beauty and the beast" as the only way to develop excellence.

I have also interviewed and fished with many business, political, sports, and community leaders who view every fly fishing experience as a potential leadership lesson. They fish for the peace, the solitude, the healing aspect of the sport, and to become better leaders.

Yes, fly fishing offers leadership lessons for those willing to listen and learn. Yet it provides so much more. As Brady Busby, fly angler, guide, and author of *Healing Waters* says, "Trout don't live in ugly places!"

CHRISTIAN BACASA
Park City, Utah

You picked up this book, and you've likely already made several correlations between fly fishing and leadership. Leaders are fervent readers and always looking to draw knowledge and insights into their personal and professional challenges. Reading often brings new insights into otherwise unfathomable problem-solving scenarios. After all, isn't that what leadership is about; "guiding yourself and others through problems?"

Leadership provides direction toward solving a problem or, more likely, a series of challenges. Often the problem is entirely new, and someone has to take the lead. Leaders are at the forefront. They experiment, ask questions, leverage other resources, and continually add to their repertoire of knowledge.

Throughout my business career, I've relied on personal experiences for inspiration and tactics. Early in my career, I learned problem-solving from rock climbing and ski mountaineering at Black Diamond Equipment Ltd. I was blessed to be mentored by former CEO Peter Metcalf, and Kim Miller, now CEO of Scarpa North America, and a countless number of other creative and inspirational members of the outdoor industry. I saw how they solved business problems like climbers solve routes. They broke things into blocks and solved each block as a simple series of micro problems.

In my mid-thirties, I faced what many consider the ultimate problem, life threatening cancer. Before that, I was a healthy, active, and passionate father and husband. Our budding family consisted of a three-year-old and one-year-old living in the mountains of Park City, Utah. The news of being diagnosed with Stage IV Hodgkin's Lymphoma was, in a way, relieving. I had been struggling to understand why I was feeling ill for so long.

After extensive treatments over the next two and a half years, I was finally facing a cancer-free future. However, I no longer had the full functionality of my lungs. My body withered to a mere ninety-seven pounds, and my strength was less than my now six-year-old daughter.

Life turned upside down. Passions like biking, skiing, and climbing were gone. My family life was under tremendous stress and disorder. My wife had taken on a workload that was unimaginable, by caring for me, our children and carrying the stress and turmoil of this disease. I needed a pattern interrupt and replacement for the activities that created such stability in my life. Fortunately, my good friends saw an opportunity. "Christian, you should join us on the annual fly fishing trip to Montana!"

I viewed fly fishing as an old gentleman's sport and thought, "Hell, I'll do that when I'm old and can no longer climb, bike and ski." Well, I was feeling old, and I had nothing to lose. Fishing wasn't new to me as I grew up in Pennsylvania, and my father often took me fishing. However, I was a bait and crankbait guy and a fly fishing newbie.

Montana often changes people, and it changed me. I got to see fishing and the outdoors from another angle. Now the rivers were a place to be excited about and not an obstacle on a climbing route. I drove to Montana and immediately found myself in a pontoon boat with a few rods and flies about which I knew nothing. Fly fishing Boot Camp had begun. All my pent up anxiety, ambition, frustration, and passion for adventure was channeled into a week of fly fishing.

You could say the trip was an effort by my friends to help with my mental and physical recovery. Everything was new, and each day I applied my problem-solving tactics to fly fishing. My mind, body, and spirit began to heal. Fly fishing does that. I then started to translate the lessons from fly fishing into my work. Breaking down leader formulas, studying river dynamics, waiting, and watching for fish activity, all of these principles I could apply to leadership challenges. Chapter one of my newfound passion was being written on that trip and little did I know it was going to be a life long journey leading to all types of opportunity, obstacles, friendships, and more.

Fly Fishing for Leadership is a personal project for John and myself. We can't express how much we would love you to share these stories, tactics, and methodologies with the people in your life.

TABLE OF CONTENTS

Foreword 3

A Message from John R Childress
and Christian Bacasa 8

Acknowledgments 17

Introduction 20

Chapter 1: Why Leadership? And Why fly fishing? 26

Chapter 2: Anatomy of a Leader 38

Chapter 3: The Foundation – Casting Skills and People Skills 48

Chapter 4: Be Here Now 58

Chapter 5: Understanding the Customer – Match the Hatch.........72

Chapter 6: Dangerous Currents 84

Chapter 7: Confidence and Belief..98

Chapter 8: Problem Solving and Your Leadership Flybox...........106

Chapter 9: Guides, Mentors and Trust 118

Chapter 10: Shadow of the Leader.......................................134

Chapter 11: Culture Matters 140

Chapter 12: Encounters That Change You 148

Chapter 13: Your Leadership Team – Fly Fishing Buddies............ 160

Chapter 14: Stewardship and Sustainability 170

Chapter 15: 50/50 and the Power of Inclusion 182

Chapter 16: Innovation – On and Off the Water.............................. 190

Chapter 17: Planning, Agility and the Unexpected 200

Chapter 18: Continuous Learning and Persistence 208

Chapter 19: Well-Being and Healing 222

Chapter 20: Stories and Communication 232

Chapter 21: Character 240

Chapter 22: It Starts and Ends with Heart.. 252

Epilogue 258

Contributors..261

About the Authors 272

Works Cited..274

Table of Contents

ACKNOWLEDGMENTS

I need fly fishing. It's a mental health imperative.
~Wade Fellin

Lots of people have contributed to this book through stories, examples, and analogies of how the principles and lessons of fly fishing shaped their understanding and practice of leadership. They are all listed in the chapter titled, Contributors. However, a few have gone above and beyond.

First, I must acknowledge Scott McEnaney, Head of Orvis Adventure Travel. Scott was generous in pointing me to the right people inside Orvis and several guides and lodge owners to get this project underway. Second, Gilly Bate, a guide and fly casting instructor whom I met by chance in the Maldives. Gilly introduced me to the UK fly fishing community to help with this book.

Christian Bacasa answered his phone one day at his home in Park City, Utah. A complete stranger from London, England asked if he would like to help with a book linking leadership and fly fishing. I found Christian, a sales executive, on LinkedIn. He is a superb fly angler who has developed a marketing and media business, with a travel booking arm for anglers and service providers, www.dupeafish.com.

Christian guided the social media and marketing of this book, as well as providing stories and behind the scenes support. As I write this, Christian and I have never physically met, but his character is evident.

We interviewed over 70 people for their stories and insights because the fly angling community cares passionately about the sport and is eager to promote it for others to enjoy. Everyone interviewed offered up two or three others. The list of contributors grew effortlessly.

Writing and publishing a book is a mystery to most of us, and self-publishing doubly so. I am grateful to Samantha Pierce, whose company (swatt-books.co.uk) helps authors with every step of the process.

We would also like to acknowledge Scott Wilday and the team at LidRig (www.lidrig.com) for their support and generous sponsorship of this project.

Finally, I need to acknowledge the generous support of Luciano Alba, owner of Estancia Laguna Verde Lodge. He helped me get out of a remote fishing location in Patagonia, Argentina, and back home as the global COVID-19 pandemic began to spread. Luciano and his staff spent hours on the phone to secure me a flight from Buenos Aires to London as the major airlines and airports were shutting down. Real leadership on their part!

Most importantly, I want to acknowledge my wife, Christiane, for supporting my fly fishing habit and helping to edit this book. A pair of non-fishing eyes reviewing a fly fishing manuscript is highly useful in pointing out leadership issues that might otherwise get lost among my enthusiasm for fly angling.

NOTE:

Those quotes in this book with names attributed are from interviews or extracted from published articles. Those quotes without a name attribution are from John Childress.

INTRODUCTION

Fly fishing is the only sport I know where you can go from Zen to total chaos in a millisecond, multiple times in a day. It's addictive.
~Richard Commodore

INTRODUCTION

The successful warrior is the average man, with laser-like focus.

~Bruce Lee

When I was eight years old, my father, the high school Principal in Myrtle Creek, Oregon, took my younger brother and me on a fishing trip to the South Umpqua River. He didn't relish the idea of taking us along. To him, getting away from his five young children, the bombardment of school administration tasks, and board meetings was his one chance for mental sanity and spiritual recovery. I suspect my mother, an English teacher, pianist, organist, plus leader of the church choir, was the deciding factor in this adventure, which turned out to be a misadventure.

I didn't know it then, but the South Umpqua River in Southwestern Oregon was, and still is, a famed salmon and steelhead river. My dad was focused on catching salmon and left us boys to fend for ourselves on the massive log jam next to the bank. The log jam consisted of old, half-submerged logs escaped from the large rafts of cut timber floated down to the sawmills in the towns below.

I was bored and encouraged my brother to follow me, jumping from log to log. Dad was at the far edge of the log jam facing the river, intent on catching a King Salmon or two for family dinners, so didn't pay much attention to us. Fly fishing takes concentration and focus, about which young, hyperactive boys know very little.

Anyway, you can probably see it coming. I slipped and fell between two large logs and let out a scream. The water was freezing. My brother Jimmy tried to pull me out, but the space was too narrow. The current constantly shifted the logs. Fortunately, my dad rescued me from drowning. To this day, I can remember the scolding, which lasted the entire drive home, about how fishing, and fly fishing especially requires focus and concentration.

They say good judgment comes from experience, and a lot of that comes from bad judgment! Definitely true for me. I am an experiential learner. When I read something, it usually goes in and out of my brain in nanoseconds. But when I experience something, it seems to stick, and I can use it to build upon other learnings.

Fast forward 22 years. I am the CEO of an international management consulting firm helping leadership teams of Fortune 500 companies focus on improving performance, usually during a turnaround or other business challenge.

One of my first assignments just a year after we started the company was to help the new CEO and management team of the Three Mile Island Nuclear Plant build a safety culture following the devastating nuclear accident the year before. What did I know about nuclear power? Next to nothing. But I did understand the power of an aligned and focused leadership team to create remarkable results. And they did. For the next 38 years, before decommissioning, TMI was one of the safest and most efficient nuclear power plants globally.

How did a guy without an MBA degree or any formal business training (my degrees from the University of California, Harvard, and the University of Hawaii were in biology, ecology, and marine ecosystems) build and lead a successful international consulting firm? Most of it comes down to the great staff and consultants we hired. Many of them were former business executives, sales executives, fighter pilots, nuclear submariners, bright young MBAs, retired Army colonels, and fly anglers. The firm stood on the shoulders of giants.

The leadership lessons I experienced as an avid fly angler (intermediate, at best, but always learning) contributed significantly to our firm's growth. You can't read about fly fishing and expect to be proficient. You have to learn the principles and lessons through experience. The same is true for leadership!

The journey of a thousand miles begins with
just a single step. ~Confucius

Leadership and fly fishing are a long game resulting from good and bad experiences and internalizing a set of core principles. Classroom lectures and endless PowerPoint slides don't create leaders; they impart information, not skills and capabilities. Fly fishing is an excellent metaphor for leadership principles, and these principles are easily transferable into the real world of work.

Policies are many; Principles are few.
Policies will change, Principles never do.
~John C. Maxwell

For example, in Chapter 2, we introduce the concept of the **Anatomy of a Leader**. In fly fishing, a tapered leader transfers energy to the fly. Similarly, the role of a business leader is to transfer energy and vision to their organization. Many other essential leadership principles have equally strong fly fishing analogies. Together, they form the backbone of this book, **Fly fishing for leadership**.

The leadership principles described in this book come from my own 40+ years of experience as a CEO, management consultant, and advisor to senior executives. Like many of you, I have read numerous books on leadership by academics, former CEOs, consultants, and leaders, both accomplished and hopeful. Each has his or her list of the characteristics that make an excellent leader. One list describes the 21 Irrefutable Laws of Leadership. It seems a little overkill to me. I have yet to meet a perfect leader in every trait, no matter what the list. But being perfect in everything is not the point. Leadership, like fly fishing, is definitely a learning journey.

Gentlemen, we will chase perfection, and we will chase it
relentlessly, knowing all the while we can never attain it. But
along the way, we shall catch excellence. ~Vince Lombardi.

I have always been impressed with the leadership principles of the United States Marine Corp. Their leadership principles are practical and realistic, which is critical when lives are on the line. And they seem to stick in people long after they retire from the military. Our consulting firm hired several former military officers, and when consulting, we often interacted with retired officers in senior management positions. To a person, they said the same thing: "Once a Marine, always a Marine."

As you read through the chapters in this book, you will notice how my take on leadership and fly fishing principles closely match the Marine Core Leadership Principles, worded differently, but the spirit is there.

Marine Corps Leadership Principles

1. Know yourself and seek self-improvement
2. Be technically and tactically proficient
3. Know your Marines and look out for their welfare
4. Keep your Marines informed
5. Set the example
6. Ensure the task is understood, supervised, and accomplished
7. Train your Marines as a team
8. Make sound and timely decisions
9. Develop a sense of responsibility among your subordinates
10. Employ your command in accordance with its capabilities
11. Seek responsibility and take responsibility for your actions

One simple reason for this similarity is that fly fishing, leadership, and the military are all hands-on activities, not spectator sports.

Along with leadership and fly fishing principles, this book includes stories, insights, and personal learnings from fly fishing guides, lodge owners, those in the fly fishing industry, and business leaders who are keen fly anglers. Also, you will find numerous inspirational business and fly fishing quotes scattered throughout.

My inspiration for this book comes from three places. First of all, my love for fly fishing and what it has taught me about life and leadership. Second from my career as CEO of an international consulting firm.

Thirdly, a conversation across a tennis net in 1980 with Tim Galway in Long Beach, California. Tim wrote the book, **The Inner Game of Tennis**, about how tennis skills teach important life effectiveness lessons and success principles. The same is true for fly fishing.

A book like this isn't for everyone. Not for every fly angler and not for every businessperson. This book is for the curious. That small percentage of the population thirsting to learn more, who constantly ask why, and are not satisfied with the status quo. Those who know there is more to experience, more to learn, and more to contribute.

Many men go fishing all of their lives without knowing that it is not fish they are after. ~Henry David Thoreau

While I have done the organization and writing, this book is a collection of the many real-life experiences of fly fishing guides, lodge owners, and business executives the world over. All have contributed to the many analogies, examples, and stories in this book. Without each of these contributors, this would be a skinny and uninteresting book.

I hope you will find at least one golden nugget of insight and inspiration to equip you on your leadership journey. For each of us, that golden nugget may be different, just as every fly fisherman has their box of "go-to" flies. Royal Coachman, Parachute Adams, Klinkhammer, Elk Hair Caddis, Chernobyl Ant, Hopper, Wooly Bugger, Muddler Minnow, Bunny Leech, Peacock Nymph, or Buzzer. All are different but effective.

Whatever insights and ideas you take away from these pages, I encourage you to use them, improve on them, and pass them along. Right now, more than ever, we need principle-based leaders as the world navigates towards a better, safer, prosperous, and more sustainable future.

"The gods do not deduct from man's allotted span the hours spent in fishing." ~Herbert Hoover

Chapter 1:

WHY LEADERSHIP? AND WHY FLY FISHING?

Fly fishing shows you life in a day.
~Gilly Bate

Chapter 1:
WHY LEADERSHIP?
AND WHY FLY FISHING?

Leadership and learning are indispensable from each other.
~John F Kennedy

*Leadership is about creating an environment where people
can be their best selves, no matter what the circumstances.*
~Stan Golub

What is leadership? There are probably as many definitions of leadership as there are different types of trout flies. And each definition tends to be fit for the specific situation and context a leader is facing. The same is true for which fly to use. It depends on the condition of the water, the weather, the time of year, the temperature, and various other factors. No one leadership approach fits every situation, just as there is no one fly for all conditions.

Yet we know good leadership when we see it. Just as we know a good fly angler we meet on the river. It's not their age or equipment, or the flies stuck on their wader patch. It's the way they behave towards the river, the fish, the environment, their dog, and their fellow anglers. I always get a sense of calm and confidence when I am around a good fly angler, and it's the same feeling I get in the presence of a good leader.

Can we learn fundamental leadership principles through fly fishing? I believe, yes!

Excellence is not a gift but a skill that takes practice. We
do not act 'rightly' because we are 'excellent.' In fact,
we achieve 'excellence' by acting 'rightly.' ~Plato

Today, perhaps more than any other time in history, leadership is required to help guide a world in crisis and chart a course for a sustainable future. Yet real leadership seems to be in short supply. There are many people with leadership roles and titles; President, Prime Minister, CEO, Congressman, City Councilor, Physician, Head Nurse, School Teacher, Parent. Yet the majority of people in the world sense a leadership vacuum. Why? What are we looking for in our leaders? I believe some of the answers lie in the principles described in this book.

We need global leaders to help focus the fight against a raging pandemic. We need CEOs who take a sustainable environment as seriously as they do share price, pre-tax profit, and quarterly returns. We need government leaders to make the careers of teachers, nurses, police, and social workers as important and financially attractive as banking and law. We need parents who teach their children the values of good leadership and stewardship, rather than abandoning them to television and computer games. I believe the world requires leaders who will work towards a better tomorrow and inspire by being role models and having the courage to make the hard decisions, not just the popular ones.

As I look through recent history, I notice that many world leaders, business executives, Pulitzer prize winners, and champion athletes were keen fishermen. A little known fact. George Washington, Revolutionary War general and first President of the United States, was, early in his career, a commercial fisherman.[1]

Herbert Hoover was known as "the fishing president" and a true conservationist. Hoover opened and expanded the number of US National Parks, including the Everglades, Great Smoky Mountains, and Shenandoah National Park. In doing so, Hoover gave anglers access to fisheries for years to come. He even wrote a book called

"Fishing for Fun: And to Wash Your Soul." In his book, Hoover famously wrote, "*All men are equal before fish.*" [1]

Dwight Eisenhower, five-star general and America's 34th President, started fishing as a young boy. After the war, he became a passionate fly angler, often spending time on Colorado's rivers. And Ted Williams, slugger and outfielder for the Boston Red Sox, was inducted into both the Baseball Hall of Fame and the IFGA Fishing Hall of Fame. Robert Redford and western author Zane Grey were both inducted into the Fly Fishing Hall of Fame.

Ernest Hemingway was inducted into the IGFA's Fishing Hall of Fame in 1998. Rick Porcello, starting pitcher for the Boston Red Sox, won the Cy Young Award in 2016. After a lackluster 2015 season, Rick spent the off-season fly fishing and getting his mojo back!

We can find leadership displayed on the battlefield, the baseball field, the classroom, the operating room, and the Boardroom. And if asked, I believe they would all say that fishing, and fly fishing, in particular, helped build and solidify their character, courage, and leadership skills.

So, how do we create more leaders? Through experience.

> *Only through experience of trial and suffering can the soul be strengthened, ambition inspired, and success achieved. ~Helen Keller*

In the middle of the Second World War, Britain was facing a shortage of young officers. The task of developing young military leaders fell to Lord Rowallan, a Lt. Col. who was then Commandant of the Highland Fieldcraft Training Centre in Scotland. The HFTC was established in 1943 to develop leadership qualities in servicemen graded "NY" (Not Yet) by the War Office Selection Boards (WOSBs) searching for potential officers.

Lord Rowallan had a strong belief that if you first develop character, military leadership skills would follow. So, he put together a ten-week wilderness skills training in the Scottish Highlands. The training at the HFTC was highly successful in developing character and leadership qualities in the cadets. The pass rate at the end of each 10-week course was about 70 percent, and most went on to be accepted by the War Office Selection Board.

The Rowallan Company was set up in 1977 in similar circumstances to address the high failure rate (70%) of officer cadets on the Regular Commissions Board. Since 1977, of the 2,900 cadets who started the courses, 65% were successful. Of the successful Rowallan cadets, 92% were successful on the subsequent Commissioning Course. Many of these reached high ranks in the service. An equally successful innovation was to admit women officer cadets to the Rowallan Company courses.

I find this approach fascinating because it was an intensive 'non-military' course designed to develop character, not military skills. Each participant took a turn at being the leader for one or more outdoor problem-solving challenges. They were graded on their effectiveness by an observing officer and by their peers. The training was filled with teamwork exercises interspersed with lectures on the character and traits of successful leaders.

I spoke with one of the former Commandants of Sandhurst, the British equivalent of West Point, who had glowing things to say about the young cadets who passed through the Rowallan program. Remember, these were the rejects, the Not-Yet Ready. He told me he would always look hard at the "Rowallan chaps" for a Cadet to head up special tasks.

Leadership cannot be taught.
But it can be learned. ~Harold Geneen

WHY FLY FISHING?

"Feedback is the breakfast of champions." ~Ken Blanchard

*What fly fishing requires is that you step into nature
and accept it on its terms. ~Tom Brokaw [2]*

As far as I am concerned, fly fishing provides almost instantaneous feedback; and plenty of it. Every cast gives feedback, every snag of a drifting nymph, every fly hung up in a tree, every day without a tug. These situations, and many more, give us essential feedback. While the average person may ignore these and mentally classify them as bad luck, the curious and determined learner will see them as opportunities to understand, rethink, re-rig, change flies, practice, and improve.

*There are no secrets to success. It is the result of preparation,
hard work and learning from failure. ~Colin Powell*

And it seems that fly fishing, on the whole, attracts a curious, thoughtful type of individual. A recent search of the Library of Congress listed 1,189 books on golf and 4,413 books written about fly fishing.

*There are certain areas that I'm pretty good at, but certain
areas that I feel like I'm just starting, which is the cool thing
about fly fishing. You're always learning. ~Tom Rosenbauer*

And fly fishing takes skill. You can't just "chuck and duck" in fly fishing unless all you want is arm exercise. Fly fishing requires a thoughtful approach since there are a hundred different things to get right to have some hope of catching a fish. And it's only through experience, feedback, and rethinking your approach that you learn to become a competent fly angler. And the same is true of leadership development. Leaders aren't born, nor are skilled fly anglers. They both develop through numerous and diverse experiences, seasoned with real-time feedback.

Finding a spot on the river that looks fishy, but is hard to reach, is an opportunity to improve. And I mean difficult. Perhaps you must wade through chest-high water and roll cast under a grassy ledge. Maybe it requires climbing over boulders and sliding down a bank where you can put your fly into a dark pool. You may have to push through tall willows and thick forest to fish a stretch of river where fish are rising just out of reach below low hanging branches you know will snag at least some of your flies.

If you embrace the tough spots on the river, a few things happen.

You build confidence. Moving around the river creates familiarity with maneuvering the unpredictable currents, rocks, and vegetation all rivers present. This translates into confidence.

You may just catch a fish. Chances are no one else has put in the work, or at least only a few. As a result, there is less fishing pressure and your odds of hooking up increase.

You push yourself a little past your comfort zone. This cannot help but make you a better fly angler. It forces you to be creative and develop problem-solving tools that will work in other, less demanding scenarios.

As you learn to read a river, there will be places that you might avoid. Don't. **Challenging yourself in fly fishing makes you better. This is true, regardless of your experience. Complacency is the enemy of progress.**

~Jason Shemchuk

Leadership and fly fishing are a curious combination of solitary and social endeavors. The classic phrase, "it's lonely at the top," not only refers to the role of the leader, but also the solitary fly fisherman out on the river. When difficulties arise, the only person you have to rely on is yourself. While a leader may consult with their team, the Board, or constituents, the final decision is theirs alone.

Out on the river, the fly fisherman can fall back on previous experiences and lessons learned from reading or talking to others. However, the final decision as to which fly, how deep to set the nymph, whether to keep fishing or head home when the storm clouds roll in, are theirs alone. And it is this reliance on self, and the courage to take the decision, that builds character and competence in both leadership and fly fishing.

Excellence in leadership and fly fishing requires a thoughtful approach, ensuring you have all the best information for making a leadership decision, and a good understanding of the river and conditions when fly fishing. Rash decisions based on gut feel or *"I saw this situation in my last company, and here's what we should do"* are often a design to fail. Fly fishing teaches us to think things through if we want to be successful. Or as Lincoln says, to sharpen the ax first.

> *"Give me six hours to chop down a tree, and I will spend*
> *the first four sharpening the ax." ~Abraham Lincoln*

Fly fishing also positively impacts our brain and biochemistry. An article about the neurobiology of fly fishing published in the Harvard Medical School, Mahoney Neurosciences Institute begins this way:[3]

In the mid-nineteenth century, the avid fly fisherman and physician James A. Hensall, MD, elucidated what for many is the allure of that often solitary form of angling. "Fly fishers," he said, "are usually brain-workers in society. Along the banks of purling streams, beneath the shadows of umbrageous trees, or in the secluded nooks of charming lakes, they have ever been found, drinking deep of the invigorating forces of nature—giving rest and tone to over-taxed brains and wearied nerves—while gracefully wielding the supple rod, the invisible leader, and the fairylike fly."

Recent research on the effects of fly fishing on well-being and quality of life among breast cancer patients comes from the Clinical Journal of Oncology Nursing.[4] Studying breast cancer patients who attended Casting for Recovery sponsored weekend fly fishing retreats showed a high degree of participant satisfaction, healing, and learning. Participants mentioned that interacting with other cancer patients, being supported by the fly fishing volunteers, group camaraderie, good nutrition, being in nature, and learning a new skill were all positive aspects of the program.

> As a critical care nurse, I have an important leadership role to help my patients during the critical period of their care. And the lessons from fly fishing have helped me immensely. The transition from beginner to expert in both fly fishing and critical care nursing goes from unsure to confident. Fly fishing has expanded my confidence. I have traveled to many countries, fished with all different types of people from all walks of life, and had the opportunity to speak up and speak out about things I believe in.
>
> *~Heather Hodson*

Humans have an evolutionary response to stress and danger, often called the "fight or flight response". A perceived or real threat causes the release of adrenalin into the bloodstream, increasing heart rate, blood pressure, and muscle tightness. Once the danger is over, adrenalin quickly disappears, and our body returns to normal, restful functioning, allowing the brain to move out of reactive mode and into thoughtful, analytical mode. During stress, we mostly react without thinking; in a relaxed mode we can think things through more clearly. If you've ever been stressed and yelled at your kids, spouse, or an employee, then a little while later realized the anger was inappropriate, you know what this is all about.

According the scientists, fly fishing is one of those activities where the body and mind can relax into an almost meditative state. Relaxation and meditation have positive, long term health benefits (for you and your relationships!). Those who fly fish take this understanding of relaxation, wellbeing and clearer thinking into their work world as well. Through fly fishing experiences, the leadership principle of slowing down, not making rash decisions, and thinking things through is more readily understood and practiced.

For me, fly fishing is a great way to reboot my overactive mind and stressful body from the pressures of leadership. I find my heart rate is significantly slower when I'm on the river. ~Brian Wetter

Fly fishing for Tarpon and handling a drift boat have both taught me a great deal about how tension and over-excitement can reduce one's ability to respond to challenging situations (like trying to land a huge Tarpon or facing oncoming river rapids). I learned pretty quickly that facing rapids with a racing heartbeat and tension greatly diminished my ability to read the river and react to oncoming dangers.

And the same is true for leadership. Getting overly excited and tense reduces a leader's ability to make effective decisions. And that nervousness gets quickly passed to employees, who then get tense, nervous, and insecure when they should be calm, clear thinking and agile in responding to a crisis.

~Chris Daughters

In these remaining chapters, you will find a series of leadership principles matched with successful fly fishing principles, using examples from business leaders, guides, lodge owners, and those in the fly fishing industry. When I first reached out to people about supplying stories and experiences for this book, nearly every individual replied, "I've never thought about fly fishing and leadership together, but I now realize there are a lot of lessons to be learned."

As a former Vice-Chairman of a global bank, investment fund manager, and seasoned Board member, I find the parallels between leadership and fly fishing fascinating. Fly fishing has both taught and reinforced my understanding and application of leadership principles. For example, three come to mind.

Expect Failure: if you expect failure, you will learn the value of patience, resilience, and humility. A key question I ask all potential leaders is: How do you react to failure? Give me an example of a failure and how you reacted.

Have a plan going in but be prepared to adapt your approach based on emerging realities. Those who chase Permit know this all too well. And those who manage people understand this principle.

Honestly evaluate the current situation – don't kid yourself about the current realities and don't underestimate the current difficulties you face. Cautious optimism is my philosophy in both business and fly fishing.

~Larry Marsiello

Diplomacy and fly fishing share many elements – patience, need for a systematic and in-depth approach, deception (oh yes! diplomats and fly anglers love it), and frequent travels. ~Stanislaw Cios

CHAPTER 1: Why Leadership? And Why fly fishing?

Photo courtesy of Aaron Smith

Chapter 2:
ANATOMY OF A LEADER

Great leaders don't tell you what to do. They show you how it's done.
~Alessandro Berselli

Chapter 2:

ANATOMY OF A LEADER

When your leader is properly balanced, you should be able to take the butt end between your fingers and cast it straight out. No line, no rod, just leader.

~A. J. McClane

Fly fishing teaches you to better understand yourself, people, and the world around you. To me that's a good foundation for leadership as well.

~Dave Engen

Developing the skills and competence for effective leadership, like mastery in fly fishing, is a long journey and the result of understanding and internalizing a set of core principles. These are not academic principles, and they are not rocket science either. Most of the time, excellence in leadership and fly fishing is applied common sense. Lectures on leadership create little impact; they impart information, but not internalized learning and capability building. Leadership principles must be experienced. Fly fishing is an excellent metaphor, and a unique sport, for understanding and experiencing the principles of effective leadership.

As a young A-10 Warthog pilot in the 81st Fighter Squadron in Spangdahlem Germany, I had a lot to learn. The aircraft systems were one thing, but there were also weapons, tactics, enemy threats, and other subjects to study and master. And then there was execution in the jet. Our main mission was Close Air Support (CAS). This involved flying formation and employing ordnance close to friendly forces to keep them safe. Fortunately, the Air Force kept some experienced pilots around to help train the new ones. The chief instructors always had one motto that they lived by, and after many years it became my job to toe the line. Humble. Approachable. Credible.

Humble. Whether it is in a drift boat, a guide shop, or back in the fighter squadron, no one enjoys feeling small when they ask a question. I always tried to remember what it was like to be the squadron's young wingman, with so much ahead of me to learn. Fly fishing can also seem overwhelming at first. Remembering that we all started somewhere helps us teach beginners. Humility keeps us from being close-minded to new ideas and techniques as well.

Approachable. You can be the best pilot in the squadron or catch more trout than anyone on the river. Still, if nobody wants to talk to you, or you are too busy to be bothered, you are not helping anyone. It was important for me to treat pilots with kindness and empathy and work to drop what I was doing to focus on those that sought advice.

Credible. At the end of the day, folks want to know that you know what you are talking about.

That could mean flying the hard missions with excellent weapons delivery or consistently catching fish and eye-watering presentation. Years in the jet, or years on the river. Both bring extremely valuable experience. In many cases, credibility is earned by admitting when you have messed up or do not know something.

Sharing our tough lessons helps others learn from our mistakes.

It may seem like a stretch, but even at the highest military aviation levels, the traits that made a good leader in the squadron translate to fly fishing.

Fly fishing can be extremely difficult to master. Only through time and persistence does one usually begin to excel. And like my career in the jet, there is always more to learn in fly fishing.

~*Jason Shemchuk*

Fly fishing takes a short time to learn and a lifetime to master. The same is true of leadership. ~Craig Langer

One of the fly fishing principles that relate directly to leadership is the ***Anatomy of a Leader***. In fly fishing, the tapered leader transfers energy to the fly. Similarly, an essential role of a business leader is to transfer energy and vision to their organization. Some even call the CEO the Chief Energy Officer.

A fly fishing leader is typically composed of three sections of different size, stiffness, strength, and length. From stiffest to most delicate, these three sections are the Butt section, Mid-section, and Tippet. Strength and stiffness differences allow for a continuous flow of energy from the fly rod to the fly during the cast. As a result, the leader perfectly straightens out at the end of the forward cast, landing gently on the water without disturbing the fish.

The **Butt Section** is the stiffest and thickest of the three, and often the shortest. It connects the end of the flyline to the variable **Midsection**, which is smaller in diameter and more flexible. The Midsection varies in length depending upon the fishing conditions. The **Tippet** connects the Midsection to the fly and usually is the thinnest. The length and size of the Tippet is chosen for the type of fly and fish targeted.

Properly put together, the tapered leader will deliver the fly to its intended target. The physics of the rod flex and the energy transfer of the leader working perfectly together.

Butt Section	Mid- Section	Tippet

Similarly, leadership has an anatomy. An effective leader possesses three distinct foundation qualities. A strong set of non-negotiable principles (Butt section), specific behaviors that fit the strategy and business context (variable Midsection), and how they treat individual employees and customers (analogous to the Tippet).

Strong, non-negotiable principles and Values	leadership practices that fit the context of the strategy and business conditions (variable)	behaviors sensitive to the specific needs of employees and customers

The Butt Section: Without strong, non-negotiable principles and values, those in leadership positions will be seen as inconsistent, bending one way or the other to improve the "optics" of their decisions. Leaders without a clear set of non-negotiable principles and values are rarely trusted by employees, customers, suppliers, and even their management team. They are tolerated but rarely win hearts and minds, nor do they last long. **One of the most critical non**-negotiable principles for leaders in today's rapidly changing world is equality and diversity of thought. An organization without an openness to new ideas and diverse points of view will find itself slow to change and embrace new business models and ways of working.

Before Douglas Conant became CEO of Campbell Soup Company, he interviewed to become a general manager at Nabisco. His final interview happened to be with Lou Gerstner, the company chairman. Conant thought it would be a formal sign-off for the job. However, it turned into a 20-minute grilling by Gerstner on all aspects of the food business. To Conant, it felt like a negative onslaught rather than an interview.

Finally, Conant had enough. "Lou, I'm sorry, but when it comes to the food industry, you don't know what you're talking about. And I don't need this job. So, if you don't think I'm the right person for it, that's fine."

Gerstner smiled and replied: "I was wondering how long it would take for you to have the courage of your convictions." The conversation took a friendlier turn from there, and Conant got the job. According to Conant, he learned a valuable lesson that day. Having a strong foundation is only half the battle. You must also have the courage to speak up and share your convictions.[5]

The Midsection: Based on the business strategy and current economic and business situation, a leader must role-model those attitudes, behaviors, and actions that support and enable the company's strategic objectives. For example, a growth strategy often requires a greater focus on sales and product development, with a greater risk tolerance. A business where safety issues can be costly and life-threatening requires the leader to actively support a safety culture; funding continuous training and team learning.

The Tippet: In addition to the non-negotiable values, behaviors, and business strategy, successful leadership requires a leader to treat employees, customers, and suppliers as individuals. The effective leader does this by adjusting his or her behavior and communications to most effectively interact, motivate, and support. Leadership requires a delicate approach and deep understanding of human motivation, plus a great deal of self-awareness on the leader's part.

> *What's an important foundation for successful leadership? Self-awareness coupled with an openness to new ideas. ~Larry Marseillo*

Of the three, I believe the Tippet is where both fly anglers and leaders make the most mistakes. It's closest to the fly and therefore closest to the fish. If your Tippet is too thick, it can scare fish and reduce your chances of the fish taking the fly. And if the Tippet is either too long or too short, it can create drag in the current or move the fly in an unnatural motion that disturbs the fish's natural feeding behavior.

Similarly, the way a leader treats an individual employee, customer, or supplier greatly impacts their effectiveness, self-confidence, and trust in leadership.

My fly fishing guiding and teaching changed almost 180 degrees after I had the opportunity to work with Mel Krieger. Mel was considered the grand master of teaching, and it wasn't just because of his fly casting abilities, which were legendary, but for his ability to connect with students. And he had a very special approach.

Mel viewed every student as a unique person, and he worked hard to understand his students as individuals through the technique of positive encouragement. Mel never used negative words with his fly casting students. Everything was positive and encouraging. And with only positive encouragement, students would relax, open up and begin a dialogue with Mel that helped to quickly identify how to improve.

~*Dusty Sprague*

In my experience, all leaders understand the importance of EBITDA, cash flow, and cost control. But few seem to realize that these are simply the outcomes of a well-run business that prioritizes innovation, effective relationships with customers, and employee development. To the business leader, innovation, customers, and employees are strategic assets for a sustainable and profitable business.

For several years I belonged to a fly fishing business owners' group where we talked about issues and challenges. What consistently came up were horror stories of how a bad guide or rude fly shop employee could negatively impact that customer for future business. And the heart of any successful business is repeat customers.

I learned that the most important person in the business is the customer, and the most important customer is the repeat customer. It's our job as leaders and guides to do whatever it takes to help that customer, whether a first timer or solid repeater, have the best experience on the water and in the fly shop as possible. To me, the business leader and the guide are equally responsible for the success and growth of the business.

~*Chris Daughters*

I find that leadership and fly fishing are a mutually reinforcing duality. Mastering the principles of fly fishing improves my leadership, and mastering the principles of leadership improves my fly fishing. ~Todd Aaronson

What has fly fishing taught me about leadership? Plenty. Most of my career in the Polish government has been as a diplomat, dealing with energy security issues affecting Poland and multilateral cooperation with the Baltic Sea countries. Good diplomacy is all about understanding the needs and motivations of others. The science and the technical issues I consider to be the basics of the job. Just like casting is the foundation for fly fishing. But real success comes from good people skills.

Like fly fishing, I must understand the current dynamics of the political situation, evaluate the motivations and objectives of those on the other side of the negotiating table, and then adapt my proposal to match them. Diplomacy includes a bit of deception, just as an artificial fly imitates the trout's real food source.

And in diplomacy, the presentation is sometimes more important than the proposed solution. My experience on the river has proven that presentation is always more important than the actual fly pattern. As long as the presentation is smooth and the line lands softly on the water, I can use just about any fly, especially a subsurface one like a nymph. And a lot of issues in diplomacy are below the surface and not openly voiced. If the presentation is natural, doesn't spook the fish and the fly acts in a normal manner, I will catch fish. And it's the same in diplomacy.

~Stanislaw Cios

Leadership is figuring out what to do when you don't know what to do! ~Michaela Merrill

CHAPTER 2: Anatomy of a Leader

Photo courtesy of April Vokey, ©Adrienne Comeau

Chapter 3:

THE FOUNDATION – CASTING SKILLS AND PEOPLE SKILLS

*Casting is the essence of fly fishing. Mastering the
art of casting allows fly fishers to enjoy the sport and
all it has to offer in all kinds of conditions.*
~Ed Jaworowski

Chapter 3:

THE FOUNDATION – CASTING SKILLS AND PEOPLE SKILLS

The most important single ingredient in the formula of success is knowing how to get along with people.
~Theodore Roosevelt

Fly-fishing, like business, was not something to do but something to master.
~Edward McVaney, retired CEO, J. D. Edwards

Seek first to understand, then to be understood.
~Stephen Covey

Fundamental, fundamentals, fundamentals! We hear that all the time in any endeavor that requires learning a set of complex skills. Success in fly fishing and leadership is dependent upon mastering multiple complex skills. Yet one can only gain mastery with a strong foundation. In fly fishing that foundation is the cast. In leadership, success rests on a foundation of strong people skills.

"As no man is born an artist, so no man is born an angler" ~Izaak Walton

With fly fishing, learning to be an accomplished caster is the indispensable foundation of this sport. Without casting skills, an angler will be limited in their ability to deliver the fly to the correct location on the water accurately and in a manner that is effective at catching fish.

Whether casting a 3-weight rod with a size 20 dry fly on a 16'
leader with a 6X tippet to softly rising trout, or punching a 12
weight rod to 100-pound Tarpon cruising directly at you into a
15-knot wind, great casting ability is crucial. The physics of the
fly rod is essentially the same in both situations. ~Dave Decker

Ed Jaworowski is one of the most influential fly casting instructors in the industry. Ed takes effective and effortless fly casting and breaks it into four mechanical principles that pertain to every cast, whether 10ft or 90ft. It's not about power and force, but about understanding the mechanics of the human body and the physical properties of the fly rod.[6]

Proper fly casting is both accurate and effortless. Good leadership is effective and effortless, and the principles of fly casting and leadership have great similarities.

If you are exhausted after a day of fly casting, you
are doing something wrong. If you are exhausted as
a leader, you are doing something wrong.

In Ed Jaworowski's explanation of fly casting, there are only two important elements, the caster, and the rod. The caster supplies the momentum, and the rod is simply a lever, focusing and delivering energy to the fly line. The same is true for leadership. There are only two important elements, the leader and people. The leader provides the proper conditions to leverage and focus the collective energy of people.

Some of you might be thinking at this point, *"Whoa! What about the wind? I cast great until the wind comes up, then it all breaks down. Isn't wind an important element?"* According to Jaworowski, it doesn't matter whether there is a headwind, side wind, or no wind; the mechanics of the cast are exactly the same. And I firmly believe that in leadership, the foundation for effectiveness is people skills, no matter who the people are, what culture they come from, or what the goal or external situation.

Ed Jaworowski's fly casting principles closely match the principles of effective leadership.

First Principle: The further you move the rod, the easier it is to cast.

A fly rod is a complicated lever, and the further it moves, back and forth, the more work it does and the more energy it creates. Short casts require little energy, long casts into a headwind require much more energy. But it's not the caster's arm power that creates the energy, but the distance the rod travels from front to back to front again.

When you move your casting hand further back behind you, you enable more energy to move the fly line. Jaworowski gives an example of throwing a baseball in his classic book, *The Cast*.

> If you throw a baseball but never bring your hand back farther, let's say, than your shoulder, you have to apply a lot of force to throw the ball. It's easier to bring your whole arm back farther and move (the ball) over an expanded distance. Do the same with a fly rod.[6]

A similar principle in leadership is the more you engage with people, the greater your leadership impact. Leadership is about real engagement with people. When the leader engages fully with employees and customers, they have more impact and more leverage to deliver results. Engagement does not mean TV commercials, Tweets, or internal company videos. Real engagement is going where people are, listening, asking for input, explaining your decisions in ways everyone can understand, and celebrating effort as well as success.

"There are only three measurements that tell you nearly everything
you need to know about your organization's overall performance:

CHAPTER 3: The Foundation – Casting Skills and People Skills *employee engagement, customer satisfaction, and cash flow. It goes without saying that no company, small or large, can win over the long run without energized employees who believe in the mission and understand how to achieve it." ~Jack Welch, former CEO of GE*

Second Principle: You can't make the cast until you move the end of the line.

Before starting the back cast, it is important to remove any slack from the line, so the back cast's energy is not dissipated before the line gets fully clear of the water. The surface tension of the line on the water and the line weight itself help load the rod on the backcast, not how much power you apply. Start with your rod tip down, next to the water, and strip in any slack line, then start your pickup for the backcast. This movement takes full advantage of the energy of the rod flex.

Equally, before a leader can fully energize a group of people towards a specific goal, there must be no uncertainty about the objective or the purpose of the effort. Uncertainty about objectives and purpose creates "emotional slack," which makes outliers to the group difficult to reach and move. Group cohesion and clarity are critical to aligning and harnessing group energy.

I always tell my students that the secret to life, and great fishing, is in the backcast. The backcast is what sets up a long forward cast, tight loop, and soft landing. And in life, the backcast is your character. Your foundation. ~Joe Dilschneider

Third Principle: Continuously accelerate, then stop the rod.

Once you pick the line up off the water, you must continuously accelerate your hand backward until you stop the rod, releasing the stored energy in the rod's flex, allowing the line to straighten out behind you. The casting motion is one continual, smooth acceleration, followed by an abrupt stop.

And similarly, with the forward cast. Smooth and continual acceleration to an abrupt stop. Don't try to punch or force the forward cast. Actually, the forward cast should take less energy from the caster than the backcast.

Effective leadership is not about forcing a group or trying to power through a challenging project. The leader is more of a guide at this point than a forcing function. Once the group has the required amount of motivation and energy, the leader needs to stop pushing. Let the group use their collective capabilities, expertise, and insights to accomplish the task. Too much instruction and pressure from the leader can easily fractionate a group and undermine their individual and collective confidence.

Fourth Principle: The line will go in the direction the tip was moving when it stopped.

Whichever direction the rod tip is pointing when you stop dictates the direction of the line and ultimately your fly. If your rod tip is out of alignment with the intended direction of the cast, then you will miss your target, either left or right.

Similarly, a group of people, and even an entire organization, is a mirror image of its leadership. If the leadership team is out of alignment, or the leader says one thing and yet continuously behaves differently, the group will be confused and find it difficult to deliver results. The fact is, people watch their leaders for clues on how they should behave. After all, very few employees or team members want to appear different from their leaders.

Want to know if you are a leader?
Turn around and see if anyone is following you!

If casting is the foundation for successful fly fishing, then people skills are the foundation for successful leadership.

Both leadership and fly fishing require active engagement.
Fish don't read memos and people don't respond
well to them either. ~Todd Desgrosselliers

One of the great questions every leader should ask themselves is: *Why would anyone follow you?* When we ask that question in senior leadership workshops, without fail, there is stunned silence. Strip away the apparent reasons that deal with authority, or payroll and many leaders struggle to come up with an answer that captures the hearts and minds of their staff and employees.

More than ever, the actions and behavior of those at the top of public, private, non-profit, and government organizations are under the massive magnifying glass we call social media. Every action and word is apt to be recorded and shared. And it is people skills or lack of, that can create a PR nightmare for the individual and the organization.

Uber founder and CEO Travis Kalanick was recorded arguing with his Uber driver and shouting about people taking responsibility instead of complaining. The video wound up on Bloomberg's business news and created a PR nightmare. Uber was already in a lawsuit with drivers over their status as independent contractors versus employees. Poor people skills on Kalanick's part eventually led to his ouster by the Board.

There is a laundry list of leadership people skills, mostly developed by consultants and academics, with everything from integrity and trust to likeability and humility. For me, and many leaders I have known over the years, the most fundamental leadership principle is respect. Respect for customers, respect for employees and their situation, their ideas, their concerns, their dreams, their struggles.

And here is where fly fishing can provide great insight into the critical leadership skill of respect. A competent fly angler respects the fish and its environment. Unless you spend time understanding the habitat, behavior, and life cycle of fish, your fishing and catching will be a comedy of errors and effort. Respect for the natural environment and the entire ecosystem of rivers, lakes, and the ocean is critical to enjoying and preserving this fragile ecosystem, which supports such great fly fishing adventures and learning experiences.

> *It's not what you accumulate during your life that matters. It's what you leave behind for the benefit of others. Both leadership and fly fishing provide opportunities to serve others and to build a legacy for future generations.* ~Todd Desgrosseilliers

The fly fishing travel business has taught me that people have the right to feel the way they do. When a trip is delayed or canceled, or the fishing conditions upon arrival are unfishable, it's natural for clients to be upset and angry. They spend thousands of dollars and wait months for the fly fishing experience of their dreams only to find the weather, travel disruptions or a global pandemic has ruined it.

By understanding that they have a right to feel the way they do, it is possible to reframe the situation. Being annoyed with their disappointment and anger just doesn't work. The same is true for any business leader when customers have a negative experience of a product or service.

I guess the lessons for me, and our travel business industry, are the critical leadership principles of compassion, understanding, and reframing. In situations where the conditions are unfishable, I always suggest a different learning experience. Maybe we can use this time to work on casting, or river craft, or learning more about the country and its people, the wine, or other resources. Leadership is about a mindset of "there is always a solution."

~Pat Pendergast

> *Fly fishing excellence, like leadership, is from the inside-out.* ~Larry Marsiello

CHAPTER 3: The Foundation – Casting Skills and People Skills

Leadership is about nudging people to improve, not demanding or ordering them. When I am with an ineffective Board, I begin by saying: "I know we can do better than this!" And more often than not, they open their minds to new and better ways of working.

~Roger de Freitas

CHAPTER 3: The Foundation – Casting Skills and People Skills

Photo courtesy of ©Marcel Siegel

Chapter 4

BE HERE NOW

Two days of focused fly fishing can feel like I've been away for a week; relaxed, refreshed and raring to go.
~Graham Ellis

Chapter 4:
BE HERE NOW

Intelligence is the capacity to be in the present. The more you are in the past or are in the future, the less intelligent you are. Intelligence is the capacity to be here now, to be in this moment and nowhere else.
~Rajneesh

Some people do yoga, meditate or attend church. I find that fly fishing helps me reach that same peaceful, centered state, and the views are better.
~Richard Commodore

I f casting is the foundation of fly fishing, then slowing down is the foundation of effective casting. Rushing the back cast or the forward cast does not allow the line to fully straighten out and correctly load the rod, resulting in a cast that often collapses far short of your target. Just about everything associated with fly fishing, leadership, and life works better when we slow down.

When I first started fly fishing, I was so excited about getting rigged up and into the water that I didn't pay much attention to what was happening on the river. I know I scared away way more fish than I caught by just jumping in, and I missed a lot of clues that could have helped me be more successful.

After about a year as a dedicated fly angler, I realized the importance of slowing down, studying the situation, the river, the weather, and the insect life for clues on how best to fish a particular area. My fishing dramatically improved, not just the number of fish but also the overall enjoyment of the whole experience.

And now that I am VP of Moonshine Rods, the lesson of slowing down from fly fishing I use every day in not rushing decisions, thinking them through, understanding the full scope of our customers' decisions, our staff, our business model. There's an old saying: "The hurrier I go, the behinder I get!" and in our business, we need to get it right for our customers, the first time and every time.

~*Tate Cunningham*

We all have stressful lives, and as women, we can get too caught up in what we're doing for everybody else. In fly fishing, you tend to slow down, take that moment, and be present. ~Jen Ripple

The flies I use for Pike are big; 16-18" in length. I use rods that have a slightly softer action, but the important thing is I need to slow the casting stroke right down, while not compromising on the power in the cast. The flies aren't overly aerodynamic, as you can imagine. They take a bit more time to get where they are going, and they also load the rod a bit slower. So, I slow my cast down, which helps the rod to load correctly. Otherwise, the whole cast just collapses in a heap.

~*Ben Bangham*

Slowing down is a fundamental principle in both fly fishing and leadership excellence. Simply, the process of slowing down helps realign not only the mechanics of casting, but also helps leaders find the right balance between pushing hard for performance and creating undue stress.

My 2015 baseball season was a massive disappointment to me. And I made it worse by putting a lot of pressure on myself to perform. The team expected great performance, the fans wanted to see strikes, and I wanted to deliver. It was not a great season, and I vowed to do better. But how? More time throwing? More time in the gym?

During the offseason, I knew I needed to regain perspective, and my "mojo". So, I went fly fishing. Over the years, I have found that through fly fishing, I could experience the value of letting go of expectations and just enjoying my fishing skills and the whole experience.

I came back to the 2016 season realigned within myself. The team and I had a great season. I won the Cy Young award, and the next year we won the World Series.

~*Rick Porcello*

As a company president, it's my job to see over the horizon and position us for the future. Fly fishing has taught me to slow down, be a keen observer and an even better listener. ~Brad Befus

There's an old saying that the riches go to those who hustle. And in many ways, business success is about speed. Speed to market, first mover advantage. Being decisive and moving forward quickly. However, quick decision making can also lead to significant mistakes and missed opportunities.

I was guiding on the Rogue River on a late-season, four-day, steelhead fishing trip through the wilderness with two large men in my boat. One of them pulled out a cigar, trimmed the end with his teeth, spit the plug in the water, and lit up. "We gotta get on the fishing pronto," he said. "We got a big pool going—"

"Let me guess," I cut in, "first fish, biggest fish, most fish—something like that?"

"Yeah. Yeah. You got it!" The man half turned in his seat, his eyes big. His voice was loud. "We gotta win that pot! Lotta dough for the taking there. We'll cut you in for a share."

As we floated downstream, I asked them a few questions about their work in the San Francisco area. They spent a good ten minutes complaining about the hectic life of driving to work in bumper to bumper traffic, and the pressure of deadlines. They said their work had turned into a perennial rat race.

I looked at them both. "Well gents, the way I see it, you have two choices, and either way, I'll bust my butt to put you onto fish. Choice Number One is you can continue to stay in your current 'rat race, full stress mode', and only focus on winning the pool money. But you'll miss what this great river has to offer. Choice Two, which I recommend, is you both slow down, step off the treadmill, and take in the beauty of this marvelous place. The leaves are turning vibrant colors in anticipation of an early frost; the big, high country bucks have started coming down into the canyon chasing the does. And the bears are in the canyon scavenging fish out of the river. We'll probably see Osprey and otters hunting for food, as well.

So, you can spend the entire trip staring at the end of your fly rod and stressing about that bet with the other guys, or you can punch out, relax, and enjoy the beauty of this wild place. Your choice."

They had a wonderful trip. We saw a lot of game along the river, they caught plenty of nice fish, and laughed most of the time. At the end of the trip, they gave me one of my biggest tips ever.

~Paul Hoobyar

Successful leadership involves seeing both the details and the big picture at the same time. And that is difficult when feeling under pressure, and one's mind is a washing machine of jumbled thoughts. Strategy, people, culture, and sustainability are not knee-jerk issues. They require a clear mind to integrate all the data and information necessary to make the right decisions.

The best sports players, for instance, seem to make decisions more slowly than their competitors. Studies of Novak Djokovic show that he waits several milliseconds longer than many of his opponents before he decides how he's going to hit the ball. By waiting that little bit longer, he is better able to choose his shot.[7]

Slow down to go fast is a good leadership principle.

And slowing down to cast further is a good fly fishing principle.

Many years ago, I attended a fly fishing lecture by an elderly English gentleman who had years of experience on the water. He told lots of good stories. In the end, someone in the audience asked him what his best advice would be for consistently catching fish. His reply was: "Attention to detail!". At that time, I didn't understand the magnitude of importance of this advice, yet many years later, I learned that lesson the hard way.

While fishing in Kamchatka for monster trout, we floated between tented camps, catching fish along the way. I was in a boat with a guide and one other fisherman when the guide said we are coming up to a great spot, so cast to the far bank, up against the cliff. Some monster fish are resting there.

I threw a mouse pattern next to the cliff face. Just as I began to strip the line in, a monster trout attacked. I saw it swirl and felt the pull, realizing it must have been close to 10 pounds, maybe more. I'm pretty experienced at fighting and landing big fish and was playing this one correctly when all of a sudden, the line went slack. Fish gone! I reeled in to discover that the knot attaching the tippet to the mouse fly had unraveled. Bad luck?

Not really. I reviewed in my mind the morning's events. When rigging up for our float, I was in a hurry, the boat loaded, and the guide yelling at us to get going. I remember quickly tying on the mouse fly and hurrying to the boat. What I didn't do was slow down and pay 'attention to detail.' I tied my fly in a hurry, and I didn't yank on it enough to secure the knot. Usually, I am calm and collected when rigging up, testing every knot, and sharpening my hook point. I can remember my grandmother saying, "haste makes waste." In this case, I wasted the opportunity to land the biggest fish of the trip.

~John Green

In Steelhead fishing, you have to do 100 things right. Doing 99 just won't get you there. In leadership, like fly fishing, it's essential not to ignore the little things, especially people's beliefs, feelings, and cultures. ~Bern Johnson

In a study of 343 businesses, those companies that developed new strategic initiatives and chose to accelerate implementation to gain a competitive edge ended up with lower sales and operating profits than those that paused at critical moments to make sure they were on the right track. What's more, the firms that "slowed down to speed up" improved their top and bottom lines, averaging 40% higher sales and 52% higher operating profits over three years.[8]

Fly fishing is a perfect stress reliever for me, and probably for many others in high-pressure leadership roles because it requires 100% focus. There's no room for negative thoughts or stress if I want to have a successful day on the water. And I am learning to bring that attitude to the pitching mound. ~Rick Porcello

Going slow to go fast is both a way of **thinking** (mindset) and **being** (behavior). These two leadership processes are combined in a simple phrase: Be Here Now.

Have you ever been speaking with someone, and after a few moments, you see their eyes glaze over, and their attention drift away? Have you ever been with someone, and you mentally drifted away? Have you ever gone home and left your brain at work? Have you ever been to a business meeting, and the speaker was the only one listening? Everyone else had their phone in their lap doing email and texting!

As jobs and lives move faster and faster, multitasking is expected, even necessary, to get work done. Yet, when people are doing one thing but thinking about another, they are generally not very effective at either. It is estimated that lack of focus during tasks and meetings reduces the average business's overall productivity by 20-40%. One of the principles recently unearthed through studies in neuroscience and human behavior is that the brain works most efficiently when it can focus on a single task for a more extended period.[9]

Successful fly fishing hinges on the smallest details; the size of the tippet, the fly's size, the pattern of fly, the accuracy and delicacy of cast, to name just a few. If any element in this chain is way off, so will be the fish. In the world of leadership and business, employee engagement, and therefore performance, are often influenced by small details as well; a pat on the back or word of encouragement for a job well done, the myriad of minor daily interactions that shape how an employee feels about a manager (and often about an entire organization). Small things matter, on the river or in the office.

~*Victor Lipman* [10]

A busy, overloaded mind causes people to miss small clues and bits of important information. Think of it as noise and interference on your mental radar screen. It's easy to miss the real information.

The most helpful information is usually on the margin, and if you are not listening fully, you will miss it. ~Larry Marsiello

I got a great job as a fly fishing guide at a top lodge in Wyoming right out of college. My classmates were all heading to jobs in banking in New York or politics in Washington, DC, but since I didn't know what I wanted to do in my life, I decided to be a fly fishing guide for a while.

One day a group of older business and government leaders showed up at the lodge, and I was assigned to guide one of them on the river. When he walked down to the boat, I almost fell over. It was Neil Armstrong, who the whole world had watched on TV, step onto the Moon. I had no idea how I would teach this famous man anything as he was already so accomplished; naval aviator, test pilot, aeronautical engineer, astronaut, and university professor.

It turned out he was not an experienced fly angler but the most intense listener and quick study I had ever met. He was humble and never tried to impress me with his accomplishments but kept asking me to show him things so he could get it right. Because of his intense focus and keen listening, he absorbed the skills of fly fishing very quickly.

I will never forget that day on the river with Neil Armstrong. What I learned watching him was the power of focus and paying attention to everything around him. I have taken that vital lesson forward into my business life, where I work hard to focus on the task at hand, especially in meetings. I pay attention to what is being said and the body language and tone of speech of others. Too many people try to multitask in meetings and easily miss important clues about people's real objectives and motivations.

~Mark George

When a person is fully present in the moment (Be Here Now), they find that subtle clues sent through gestures, facial expressions, posture, voice tone, and emotional energy are easily picked up. Since non-verbal gestures carry more than half of human communication and engagement, it is essential to focus and not multitask.

Fly fishing has been tremendous in improving my leadership capabilities. For years I have been a member, and at times Chairman, of government-sponsored working committees to assess and improve policies for the regulation and protection of wild salmon in Scotland. Reaching sound policy decisions by committee (made up of individuals with sometimes wildly different agendas) requires exceptional leadership skills to productively engage all members in a constructive and purposeful debate based on the available scientific facts. It also requires that every participant feels valued for their concerns and able to participate fully.

And that's where my years of fly fishing for trout and salmon come in. For me, fly fishing the rivers and streams of Scotland and England provide the ability to clear my mind of multiple and often competing issues and focus on one thing at a time. Successful fly fishing requires that kind of focus, from reading the water to choosing the right leader, fly, and making an effective presentation. It's impossible to do that successfully with a cluttered mind.

Having learned from my fly fishing experiences, the value of focus when making decisions has been a tremendous aid to me in helping government committees reach sound policy decisions that make a positive difference.

~*Richard Sankey*

The practice of Be Here Now helps us listen to what is being said with an open mind, rather than our mind occupied with judging whether the content is right or wrong.

I love teaching women to fly fish. They listen better, don't feel the need to compete like men do, and ask good questions that help everyone engage and learn. ~Christine Atkins

Be Here Now is about focusing to understand the meaning behind the words and not just the words being spoken. This way of listening allows you to step into the other person's shoes and see their point of view; a critical leadership trait.

Watch a professional guide or angler approach a promising stretch of water, and the first thing they'll do is stop and watch. Nothing should be assumed at this point, and yet everything you've learned as to where trout hold and why should be considered. ~Craig Fellin

Psychologists Mihaly Csikszentmihalyi and Jeanne Nakamura call the mindset of focused attention "Flow State," which describes how individuals feel when they are fully immersed, mentally, and physically in whatever you are doing.

There's this focus that, once it becomes intense, leads to a sense of ecstasy, a sense of clarity. You know exactly what you want to do from one moment to the other; you get immediate feedback. ~Mihaly Csikszentmihalyi [11]

When your full attention is on an activity or task, especially one you are passionate about, you create the conditions necessary for a flow state of mind in which everyday mental chatter fades away, and you become fully absorbed and focused. Interestingly, flow state is less common during physical relaxation but is present during challenging and stimulating activities. In terms of performance and positive feelings, the best moments in our lives occur when mind and body are stretched to accomplish something worthwhile.

And fly fishing is a good example. Everyone has made a perfect cast, often more than once. When that happens, the feeling is both euphoric and effortless. Yet how many of us do it every time?

We know we can make a perfect cast, but not every cast is perfect. Why? Often the problem lies in our mind and not our casting muscles. The more mentally distracted you allow yourself to become, the less you can activate your full potential. This certainly shows up in tennis matches when a player starts overly worrying about losing the point or double-faulting on the serve.

> *Don't get rushed into a decision as a leader. Take the time to think things through. And as a fly angler, don't strike too soon, let the fish hook itself otherwise you risk pulling the fly out of its mouth. Just as you risk a poor business decision by reacting too quickly. ~Clement Booth*

And in fly fishing, the mental interference caused by worrying about the wind, the trees behind, or trying extra hard to force a long cast, often results in poor performance. The same applies to leadership. When an executive is faced with a difficult decision or a potential confrontation with an angry client or customer, the mental interference of worry, or fear of making a mistake, results in a less than satisfactory outcome.

> *Concentrate all your thoughts upon the work at hand. The sun's rays do not burn until brought to a focus. ~Alexander Graham Bell*

2004 was my first-time fly fishing. My brother is a keen fly angler and kept bugging me to join him on one of his trips. I finally relented, took a weekend class from Orvis, and joined my brother and a guide on a float trip.

What got me hooked on fly fishing was being out in remote places, disconnecting from my busy life as a partner in a global management consulting firm, and enjoying solving the myriad of challenges and choices associated with effective fly fishing.

The experience of intense focus, being fully present in the moment, and keenly attuned to everything around me was profound. Since then I have worked hard at giving 100% focus and attention in my work, meetings, and with everyone I spend time with.

~*Sean Monahan*

It's dark because you are trying too hard. Lightly child, lightly. Learn to do everything lightly. Yes, feel lightly, even though you're feeling deeply. Just lightly let things happen and lightly cope with them. ~Aldous Huxley

As a young fly fisher, I often repeated a fundamental mistake. On seeing a tangle in my leader, I would try to fix it in a hurry by false casting frantically. I eventually learned this hasty approach never works. The worst thing to do with a beginning tangle is to wave it around and try to muscle it free. It almost always makes it worse. It is better to take it slow, figure out which part of the tangle is the best place to start, and then tease out the tangle.

The same lesson applies when I encounter tangles in running an international environmental law organization. Rather than jumping in and trying to muscle up a hasty solution, it works much better to listen first, pay attention to all the issues, and identify the root of the problem. By slowing down and listening respectfully, I can often find the one insight that helps unravel the whole problem.

~*Bern Johnson*

I like fly fishing because it gives me a chance to switch off the "washing machine noise" in my brain about all the business challenges I have to solve. And while I focus 100% on the full immersion experience that is fly fishing, there is a part of my brain that continues running subroutines in the background. At the end of the trip, I usually come out wholly refreshed and with new insights and solutions. ~Graham Ellis

Chapter 5:

UNDERSTANDING THE CUSTOMER – MATCH THE HATCH

Leaders start with the customer and work backwards. They work vigorously to earn and keep customer trust. Although leaders pay attention to competitors, they obsess over customers.
~Jeff Bezos

Chapter 5:

UNDERSTANDING THE CUSTOMER – MATCH THE HATCH

We're not in the coffee business serving people. We are in the people business serving coffee!
~Howard Schultz, Starbucks

It's the client's goal that I must focus on and that should stay constant. My guiding plans and approaches will change depending upon the circumstances of the day."
~Capt. Skip Zinc

As a fly angler, one of the core skills I had to learn to be successful was to read the river, study the current and structure to locate good fish areas, and cast to them.

Equally, in my business life, it was important for me to learn how to read the market, find opportunities and understand customer preferences to successfully grow.

~Jen Ripple

To have a high probability of catching fish, it is important to understand the fish's many habits and behavior. Fish are voracious feeders, but they can also be very selective. Similar to a retail customer, liking only one color of shoe and not another.

No two rivers are the same, just as no two companies are the same,
even in the same industry. It's important for me to approach each
with an open mind, yet draw on my database of experiences to quickly
read each new situation to find the best approach. ~Mark George

It was a classic mayfly day on the legendary Test River in England, and the *Ephemera danica* were everywhere in the air. It promised to be a magical day for my client, yet the rising fish refused her expertly presented fly all morning. There were two constantly rising fish that ceremoniously refused every one of my favorite mayfly patterns. I kept switching different patterns, colors and sizes, without success.

Exasperated at not getting my client into fish, I suggested we sit for a while and observe what was going on with these fish, who were actively feeding off the surface. I was captivated by the mass of mayflies in the air all around us and convinced I just hadn't found the right Mayfly pattern yet. We tried some other patterns, fished for a little while longer, but still refusals.

Then it dawned on me that I was assuming the trout were feeding on mayflies because so many were in the air. What if it was something else? I lay down on the grass so that I could look just above the surface. It was a cold, windy, damp day, but I desperately needed a different perspective on this problem.

That's when I realized the trout were feeding, not on Mayflies, but on a Mayfly cousin, the Iron Blue (Alainites muticus), a small upwing that likes cold, windy conditions for hatching. We changed to an Iron Blue emerger pattern and started catching fish immediately.

This experience took place in my early days as a professional guide. Having gained several years of experience, my approach to a river is now different. Instead of just drawing on my memory about trout and their typical feeding habits, I take the time to look at the situation and the fish's behavior on that day from different angles. Trout may be predictable in their feeding habits, but every situation is different, and fish, like customers, will often surprise you.

~*Gilly Bate*

Every serious fly fisher takes time to learn at least a little about the biology, ecology, and behavior of the fish species they are after. It just makes good sense to understand as much as you can about the fish. Many books delve into the biology, habit patterns, and ecology of trout, salmon, and other gamefish species. But it is also essential to supplement your book learning by asking questions of your guide, lodge owner, and fellow fishing partners. Knowing as much as possible about the fish is a great help in success on the water. You might call it "ichthyopsychology." [12]

A guide once told me that to understand fish; you only need to know three things about them. They are always looking for food, are concerned with energy management, and want to feel safe. With that understanding, I began to read the water better and understand where the fish would likely be holding and how to best entice them.

And that lesson was not lost on me as a management consultant either. Clients have needs, and to help them and their business, I needed to figure out what was important to them. Yes, they wanted the problem solved or costs reduced, but there are human needs as well, and as a project leader, it's my job to understand that.

~*Sean Monahan*

Every new day brings a different set of circumstances that impact where, when, and what fish are feeding on. Thus came the concept of choosing a fly pattern that closely resembles what the fish are currently feeding on, which is thoroughly discussed in the 1997 classic book by Pat O'Reilly, *Match the Hatch*.[13]

I learned to fish from my father as a way to eat. We would go camping and brought along fly rods so as not to carry so much food. My father always caught more fish than my brothers and me. He was a proficient fly angler, yet he only fished dry flies. In trying to emulate his successes, I taught myself to fish with only dry flies. I didn't know any other reality. Although I enjoyed many successful outings over the years, big fish tended to escape me unless I was absolutely in the right place at the right time.

Many years ago, I went fly fishing with my good friend, Michael Marx. I was catching several nice sized fish, but Michael was catching lots of big fish. It didn't take me long to realize that much of his success came from nymph fishing. He went to where the fish were instead of trying to entice them to the surface. It is exciting to catch big fish on the surface and entice them with a perfect drift. His approach was more successful, because he understood that fish exist in an entire biological and hydrological ecosystem, and one needs to go where the fish are.

Highly effective leaders understand people and organizations much the same way. They recognize they exist inside a much bigger ecosystem. Inside the organization, this ecosystem includes people, processes, technology, and culture. Outside the organization, their ecosystem consists of customers, communities, societies, and the environment. Like good fly anglers, good leaders understand these interconnections and vary their approaches accordingly to create business success without negatively impacting that delicate balance.

~Scott Pope

The parallels between fly fishing and leadership are numerous, especially about dealing with customers, employees, suppliers, and other stakeholders. Without an understanding and respect for people, business success is short-lived at best. And without an understanding and respect for fish and their environment, fly angling becomes a frustrating hassle.

Fly fishing is like running an On-line business. Most of the time, you never see your customer, and you don't see the trout most times either. So, a quality presentation is everything in fishing. And customer service and product quality are the keys to success for an On-line business. In my business, Barbless Flies, I stress customer service and quality. We put a hand-written thank you note in each order, and shipping is free, anywhere in the world, whether the order is 3 flies or 300. And our repeat business is 80%, while in most On-line enterprises, only 25% of business comes from repeat customers.

Treat customers fairly, make them feel special, and they will come back for more. And the catch and release ethos of fly fishing is the same. That's why we only sell barbless flies. We want that great fish you just caught to reproduce, and live a long life for other fly anglers in the future.

~*Richard Fieldhouse*

In my opinion, too many guides have a set pattern for fishing, and as soon as they meet their client, they start their standard presentation on how best to fish the river. It usually goes something like this: *"I've fished this river many times and know exactly how it should be fished. So, here's what you're going to do…"*. And more often than not, the client follows directions. Yet what about the client's needs?

Many guides miss an essential element of their craft. Asking the client what they want from the day! My guides and I developed a habit, even before we get the client onto the water, of sitting down with them, pouring a cup of coffee, and asking about their objectives for the day. Is it to catch lots of fish? Great. Is it to improve their casting ? Is it to heal themselves through an enriching experience in the wilderness? Every person has a different reason for going fishing, and it is important for the guide to find that out early on and help them achieve their objectives.

And I believe this is a powerful leadership principle as well. Every employee has a different reason for going to work, and it is poor leadership to assume everyone has the same work goals. For some, it's all about security and paying the bills. For others, it's the opportunity to develop their skills further or gain money, recognition, or promotion. An engaged workforce is one where people can realize their personal and professional objectives, and as a result, they give additional effort beyond a paycheck.

A fly fishing client who achieves their objective for the day will walk away from the river with a full heart and unforgettable memories.

~Pete Tyjas

It's all about the client,
not the guide's ego.

My biggest mistake as a rookie guide was to talk about politics and voice my personal opinions with a client. And I learned that lesson the hard way.

Our lodge had a group of clients from Texas, obviously very successful, who came to stay and fish every year. I was a reasonably rookie guide and took them out on the river. I knew a lot about fly fishing and the river, but very little about dealing with clients.

They were a lively group and loved to talk about cars and the good old' days in college. I assumed they were in the oil business, and since everyone was opening up and have a good time, I brought up how terrible Fracking was and how it was ruining the groundwater and causing earthquakes. The day suddenly turned cold, and it wasn't the weather.

We finished the day in silence, and that group has never come back to the lodge.

My ego caused us to lose a large group of paying clients, and the income loss impacted the dishwashers, the maids, the cooks, everyone. I learned a valuable lesson that day. It's all about the clients having a fulfilling fishing experience, and my job is to support that. Period!

~Wade Fellin

People will give you what you want, if you first give
them what they want. ~Thomas D. Willhite

So, the leadership question is: How much do you know about your customers? How much customer data do you gather? How do you use this data? How often do your senior executives work on the front line to have real customer contact?

*Quality in a service or product is **not** what you put into it.*
It is what the customer gets out of it. ~Peter Drucker

There is an old story told in most marketing classes that illustrates the importance of understanding the customer. Probably more apocryphal than real.

A dog food manufacturer wanted to grow its market share and hired the best animal nutritionists, food chemists, package designers, and product marketers. They spent thousands of working hours and millions of dollars to develop the very best dog food on the market. Two months after the launch, sales were not only flat but well below projections.

The CEO assembled the entire team for a review and demanded to know what was wrong. The experts were adamant that they had created the most nutritious dog food, the best packaging and labels, and the most sophisticated data-driven marketing campaign. Towards the end of the meeting, the secretary taking notes raised her hand and said, "My dog doesn't like it! And my neighbors say the same thing!"

It's not how beautifully tied your flies are, or how expensive your rod and waders. It's all about the fish, not you! Effective fly fishers take time to understand the habits and behavior of the fish. Effective leaders focus the organization's attention on understanding the needs and wants of their current and future customers. They listen, observe, and ask questions. They want to know why!

> *I go to the river the same way I go to work. With a goal*
> *in mind, but before I do anything, I spend time observing,*
> *gathering information and data, and think about the*
> *best way to approach the situation. ~Bob Mallard*

My first fly fishing trip to Chile was in 1997 where I met John Jenkins, at the Heart of Patagonia Lodge on the Rio Aysen, nestled among some of the best trout water in the world. As a young, rambunctious fly fishing guide in Alaska, I was used to throwing big streamer flies, mouse patterns and drifting egg patterns for voracious fish which were not wary or leader shy. They were bulking up for the long winter, and it was not really technical fishing. In Chile, however, the fishing was very technical, and presentation was everything.

After several hours of showing off my monster casts and flogging the water with no success, John pulled me aside and gave me some very blunt and beneficial advice. His advice was to approach the water with curiosity. Learn all that was going on at this particular spot. Look for holding water, look for structure and pockets, look for insects, hatches, and rising fish. And then he got specific. He told me to get out of the water (we Alaskan fly fishers like to wade deep) and start with a short 10 ft cast, then progressively move my cast out further and further as I learned how the fish were responding. I did as he said and started catching fish.

John's advice works for fly fishing and business as well. First, learn everything you can about the market, your customers, your competitors. Learn what works then move out progressively. Don't build a moon-shot plan at the beginning. Wait until you understand all the dynamics, have all the capabilities at hand, and then go for the big score.

~Pat Pendergast

There is no such thing as an unimportant piece of customer information and insight.

The managerial equivalent of matching the hatch is what I call "the motivational hatch". A manager needs to understand what most motivates employees and then "match" their needs with appropriate policies, recognition, and incentives. Motivations are as individual as personalities. Some employees want praise and recognition, others seek more time for family and better work-life balance, some may be lured by titles and corner offices, while still others may care for little beyond compensation and bonus. As on the river, it's up to a manager to crack the code and determine what will most motivate.

~Victor Lipman

Productivity requires having the right tools and equipment, as well as skills. But a large part of employee productivity is also determined by individual motivation. Leaders continuously search for the right motivational elements, usually landing on compensation, promotions, or interesting and challenging work. Yet to apply all the various motivational elements equally across a group of employees is not universally effective. The reason? Each individual is motivated by different external elements, plus their internal motivational drivers.

Matching the "motivational hatch" can be very different from employee to employee. And part of success in business, or any other situation with people working towards a goal, is to understand as much as possible about individuals' motivations. Like finding the right fly, this is not always easy and does take time, but the results definitely pay off.

As a young, hot-shot guide I was part of a two boat trip with lodge clients in each boat. In one boat was the lodge owner acting as guide, with my clients in the second boat. Both boats left at the same time, but I got way ahead and fished my clients hard. I was determined that our boat would catch the most fish, and I urged them to keep fishing the entire day. We arrived back at the lodge an hour after our designated meeting time. But we had a killer day on the water. Or so I thought.

Arriving at the lodge bar, my clients were exhausted and said very little, while the other boat crew was laughing and talking about the great day they had. When I asked, rather smugly, how many fish they caught, they said none. They spent the day exactly as they wanted, sightseeing and stopped early to go into town to see the sights and do some shopping.

It hit me like a ton of bricks. My trip was all about me, and my objective was to show off and be the boat with the highest fish. I never even thought of asking the clients what their objectives were for the day. I got a terrible review of my guiding, but learned a valuable lesson.

As a business owner, I am now very aware of asking customers and employees their objectives. What they want to learn. What new skills they would like to develop. I listen, and then work to provide them with the support and opportunities to achieve their goals. The way I see it, when they win, our company wins.

~Oliver White

An interesting element of a business is that customer needs and behaviors change over time. When technology advances and brings in new products with greater value or convenience, customers quickly shift their buying preferences. Many of us used to make the weekly trip to the DVD rental store to return and stock up on new movies until streaming technology made consuming video content as easy as using a remote control in your living room. As a result, Netflix flourished, and Blockbuster went bust.

No two rivers are the same, just as no two companies are the same, even in the same industry. I need to approach each with an open mind yet draw on my database of experiences to read each new situation to find the best approach. ~Mark George

Photo courtesy of Gibson Pictures, iStock

Chapter 6:

DANGEROUS CURRENTS

Both leadership and fly fishing are going to seriously test your resolve.

Chapter 6:

DANGEROUS CURRENTS

When you take confidence to a dangerous level, you begin to overlook the small signs of slipping performance, which slowly compound into an eventual disaster.

Most of my mistakes in business and fly fishing are the result of rushing into the situation without stopping to assess things properly.

~Clement Booth

Fly fishing has taught me some great lessons; many of which have come from dangerous situations I got myself into. For me, fly fishing is about adventure more than relaxation, and I tend to push the envelope sometimes.

As a rather novice fly angler I was so excited fishing one afternoon that I suddenly realized it was almost dark and the light was fading fast. Yet here I was in the middle of a river of large rocks and boulders covered with slippery moss. And without a flashlight!

I gingerly made it back to the bank in the dark and slowly followed the trail back to my car, tripping over a few logs and taking a few wrong turns as well. That taught me a great life lesson about being observant and fully aware of my surroundings. I now notice every fern, mushroom and fallen logs along trails and even though I am concentrating on my fly I am now keenly aware of the weather and time of day.

For me, being totally aware of things going on around me is a leadership principle as well. Too many leaders have a narrow focus during a meeting or team discussion and miss the non-verbal signals and clues from other's behavior. It's easy to get lost in your own conversation or agenda and miss some important insights and information.

~April Vokey

Fly fishing and leadership are not just about trophy catches and soaring share prices. There are hidden dangers in both. Successfully dealing with threatening circumstances, whether a tricky river current or sudden business turbulence, is a critically important skill. Believe it or not, people die from fly fishing accidents and have significant complications, like eye injuries and broken bones.[14] We definitely need to respect the water, the outdoors, and sharp hooks!

Business success is not guaranteed either, even for large Fortune 500 companies. Comparing the 1955 list of *Fortune 500* companies to the 2017 *Fortune 500*, there are only 60 companies that appear in both lists. In other words, fewer than 12% on the 1955 list are still on the Fortune 500 list 62 years later. And 88% of the companies from the 1955 list have either gone bankrupt, merged with or were acquired another firm, or have fallen from the top *Fortune 500* companies.[15]

Three characteristics that create and exacerbate dangerous situations in both leadership and fly fishing are hubris, poor self-awareness, and overconfident risk assessment. The fly angler who doesn't understand or respect their own physical limitations or doesn't understand the various risks involved in flying fishing can easily find themselves in a serious situation. And in most cases, the river or the ocean is not your friend.

We wade into deep water in our work lives. We put our all into what we do every day. Holding on to a perfect cast, a fish brought into the net, can help us weather the other parts of our work lives. Especially when we run into those parts of life that are less than perfect. ~Brian Childress

And the same principle applies to those leaders who don't understand or respect the limitations of their organization or competitors' capabilities. A simple example is developing a winning go-to-market strategy that employees can't deliver on. The strategy may be well-conceived, but employees don't have the required skills, knowledge, or capabilities to deliver. The result is increased costs, loss of market share, and shortly, a new CEO.

If you ask me why CEOs and leaders fail, I would say it's often the result of four issues that compound each other.

The first is that they are excellent at one function or skill (sales, finance, engineering, etc.) but don't expand their knowledge base to encompass enterprise-wide issues and understanding how the various pieces of the organization function and work together.

Second, they fail to surround themselves with people who know more than they do. And this is common with leaders new to an organization and feel they have to prove how smart or capable they are.

Third, they fail to share power and give recognition and control to others, thus reducing motivation and innovation.

The fourth may be the most damning of all. Too much focus on planning and goal setting, and not enough on actual execution.

~Larry Marsiello

Larry Marsiello and I fished in the Caribbean islands of Los Rochas, Venezuela, several years ago, and he is a highly successful business leader and keen fly angler. If you think about it, his four points above apply to fly fishing as much as they do to leadership.

There is rarely the luxury of time to work out detailed plans in high stress or high-risk situations. Think of a fighter jet in a dogfight or turning around a nearly bankrupt company. Time is not your friend; quick decision-making is required. It is essential to eliminate potentially harmful decisions and errors to find a decision that gives the highest probability of success. And then you need to do the same thing over and over again. This approach to rapid problem solving was developed by the German philosopher Karl Propper, and I use it whenever approaching a difficult problem.

And success in fly fishing is the result of quick decision making about which fly and what style of presentation to use before the fish gets spooked. You only have a short window to get the fish to strike, so it is important to learn what doesn't work, eliminate that, and try another approach. And good problem solving is not based on random trials, but using past experiences and knowledge gained from time on the river, or in the cockpit of a fighter jet, or leading a business.

~Gordon Sim

Leaders make mistakes, and failure is part of every leader's life. But how you handle the aftermath of an error is critical. Great leaders quickly learn from mistakes and develop plans, approaches, and actions to handle the situation differently in the future.

Wading is probably the most dangerous of all activities in fly fishing. Boulders, sudden holes, and rocks covered in slippery moss litter the river bottom. And if your waders fill with water, it makes walking and floating nearly impossible for the average person.

I was a novice fly angler, but a confident businesswoman when I first fished the Ballindalloch beat on Scotland's Spey River. I was happy, standing knee-deep on the pebbly bottom, water clear and fast, air warm and still. It was almost Heaven, marred only by a couple on the opposite bank trying to untangle their lines and arguing loudly about who hadn't packed the right reel, leader, or flies. I tried to blank out their voices ruining the peace of a perfect morning's fishing.

Soon I was into a nice fish and looked around for my ghillie, thinking he'd net it more safely than me. However, he was on the opposite bank, helping the squabbling couple. I tried shouting at him, but the rush of the river was too loud.

I thought if he can cross the river, so can I. So, I started into deeper water, my fish still secure, my rod aloft. I was nearly half-way across when I realized the water was too strong and inches from flooding my chest waders. I made a hasty backward retreat, heart pounding, legs flailing.

My fish stayed on the line and as I got back to the bank the ghillie walked across on the underwater quoins previously built to cross the river -- which I'd not seen. He got his net down for my salmon, but after being played for so long, it came off the hook and leapt for freedom. On reflection, I was fortunate to lose just the fish and not my footing or my life.

With no knowledge or evidence, making a decision, like how or where to wade across the Spey, is unwise. Taking prudent risks is important in business, and prudent is the keyword. A bit of research, forethought, and input from experts are required for successful fly fishing, and business.

~Prue Leith CBE

Tom Melton was a relatively inexperienced fly fisher on a bucket list trip with a friend to one of Chile's famous brown trout rivers when he had to wade across a river for the first time. Needless to say, it was a nerve-racking experience. Afterwards, his guide shared with him five important rules of wading. Being an experienced businessman and leadership consultant, Tom thought long and hard about those rules and translated them into leadership principles when facing uncertain and potentially dangerous business situations.[16]

Look before you leap. It is important to avoid rushing in and thinking that this particular river (business challenge) is the same as many you've seen before. The reality is, every river bottom and current flow is different, just as every business challenge is different. Study the river carefully (unless you are being chased by a bear and about to become lunch, then run like hell). Also, have a clear view of the goal, or end in mind. Where exactly on the opposite side of the river, do you want to wind up? Likewise, in business, take time to gather information about the situation and determine the desired outcome.

One step at a time. With each step, analogous to each business decision, stop and evaluate the situation. Also, take time to regain your balance and bearing. Each step provides you with meaningful feedback about the conditions of the crossing, and the business context. Make certain you have a firm footing before moving forward.

Pay attention to the currents. In a river, much like a business environment, there are many currents and eddies. And they shift continuously. However, a river has a rhythm, an ebb, and flow that, if you pay attention, can show a distinct pattern, similar to the pattern of the surf where every 7th wave is the biggest.

Likewise, there are currents of energy and emotion inside every business, which ebb and flow from a combination of internal and external events. Suppose a leader is not tuned in to the moods and culture of the organization? In that case, they will miss a critical part of the decision-making process, which considers whether or not the organization is capable of executing the task at hand.

Ask for help. Too many leaders see themselves as the hero whose role it is to have all the knowledge and expertise to solve any problem. To them, asking for help is a sign of weakness! One of the ground rules for wading across an unfamiliar river is to ask for help from the guide. All guides want a safe outing for their client. Locking arms while wading across a river is not a sign of weakness, but wisdom. And if there is no guide available, think twice, and if you must cross, use one or two wading staffs for balance and security.

Don't panic if you slip and fall. Before any wading activity, a competent guide will check that your wader belt is tight around your waist as a precaution against water filling up your waders. There is enough air in the waders with a tight belt to help you float, so go with the flow. Keep your head and feet up. Use your feet to bounce off rocks as you float downstream and look for a spot on the shore where you can paddle toward, and eventually climb out. This is an excellent leadership principle when a crisis hits. Don't panic, keep your head up, collect as much information about the situation as you can, and look ahead for a way out.

~Tom Melton

Over time, every leader experiences failure, just as every fly fisher gets dunked once in a while. And slipping and falling in the river is a perfect opportunity to learn. Instead of drying off and getting right back at it, it is a good practice to take some time out to reflect. Don't discredit your failures and falls so quickly. Lasting lessons can be learned that will strengthen you to handle similar situations better next time.

The military has a process called the *After-Action Review* [17] and is religiously followed. Lessons learned from a past situation can spell life or death the next time around. And a good fly fishing guide will spend time with a client after a fall or an accident to cement the lessons learned.

In my military experience, the After-Action Review is one of the best leadership development tools. ~Don C. Puckett

Highly successful business leaders make the After-Action Review mandatory after every marketing campaign, every product launch, every strategic planning review.

When you react, the event controls you.
When you respond, you're more in control.

There are sudden, unforeseen dangers in fly fishing, and also in the business world. The recent global COVID-19 pandemic is a good example. Trying to power through a crisis in business-as-usual mode is usually not the answer. When the situation is far from normal, previous budgets and goals need ditching so that resources are reallocated where they will do the most good.

As a fly angler, I am familiar that a sudden shift in weather or river conditions requires a wholesale change in approaching the day's fishing. As a CEO, recognizing the signs of fundamental change in an industry or the economy before it's too late is a critical leadership skill.

I spent much of my business career in the hospitality industry and have experienced the devastating impact of an economic downturn resulting in a significant reduction in leisure travel, families eating out, and reduced business travel. All of which hit the hospitality and retail industries before the rest of the economy.

When we first heard about COVID-19 in late December, we paid close attention. In late February, I met with city and civic leaders, suggesting that it would soon hit our small community with devastating economic impact. Most took the news lightly, and few made disaster plans.

In my organization, we immediately began contingency planning, talking to staff about all the potential problems and changes in working conditions and schedules. We got everyone engaged in scenario planning not only for their jobs but also for their families. As a result, we did have furloughs and layoffs, but the staff were prepared, expected it, and had their lives well planned.

~Todd Aaronson

Fly fishing teaches many lessons about changing plans and approaches, yet there is a strong resistance among senior management to change policies, work processes, annual budgets, and objectives in business. As we quickly learn in fly fishing, unwillingness to change is a design to fail.

Leaders also face strong currents in emotionally charged issues, especially with disappointed clients or high visibility, costly internal projects that fail to deliver. These are dangerous currents and tricky to maneuver.

A bad leader can ruin a good company faster
than a good leader can turnaround a bad company.

The most dangerous person on the river is the fly fisher who fishes maybe once or twice a year, in exotic places, and thinks because he's fished in Kamchatka or Alaska, that he knows it all. The most dangerous person in business is the executive who thinks he knows it all and tries to micro-manage situations and make every decision.

> Neither of these two characters listen, and therefore rarely learn or improve.
>
> *~Mark Thompson*

Nearly 1,500 CEOs left or were removed from their jobs in 2018 (according to a report by outplacement firm Challenger, Gray & Christmas) [18]. While a quarter of these departures were classified as retirements, many left due to an inability, or reluctance, to adapt to major industry disruptions, new technologies, or new competitors. In many ways, disruption from external forces is a significant danger for a business leader who won't acknowledge the possible impact of new ideas or innovations on their industry or company.

In 2000, a young technology entrepreneur named Reed Hastings approached John Antioco, CEO of Blockbuster, then the dominant force in the movie rental industry with 9,000 stores globally and nearly $6 billion in revenue, about acquiring his startup, a movie rental company called Netflix. Antioco refused.

Just seven years later, Antioco was fired, and Blockbuster was bankrupt by 2010. At that time, Netflix had revenues of $2.5 billion and on its way to becoming a major force in paid content streaming and movie production.

The greatest danger in times of turbulence is not the turbulence;
it is to act with yesterday's logic – Peter Drucker

Another danger to both fly anglers and business leaders is complacency. We can keep doing those things that made us successful only as long as the business environment and the river stay the same. But the business landscape and the river are always changing. To fall asleep at the wheel with illusion that success is a given is an invitation to disaster.

I was fishing one of the high mountain lakes in the Cascades of central Oregon for large trout. It was a good day fishing, and I could feel myself getting complacent with my success. I set my rod down on the edge of the boat and turned around to talk to my buddy about how we were crushing it today. A few seconds later, my brand new Sage rod and reel went screaming out of the boat, skipped across the water for 30 yards, and sunk into the depths.

That expensive and painful lesson stays with me as a reminder in both fishing and business about becoming complacent from success. Effective fly fishing and leadership are about being alert for any and all eventualities.

~John O'Connor

Jim Collins, author of the best-selling business book, ***From Good to Great***, also wrote a less well known book, ***How the Mighty Fall***,[19] which describes the typical stages in the decline of companies once at the pinnacle of success, which then fell into irrelevance. His research follows the decline of once-great companies such as Bank of America, Motorola, Circuit City, Fannie Mae, Zenith, and the A&P grocery chain. It is easy to add Lehman Brothers, General Motors, and the UK's largest construction company, Carillion, to this list, which is by no means exhaustive.

Collins defines the first stage of business decline as hubris. In other words, the attitude that future success is expected and guaranteed because of past achievements. Such arrogance and complacency often make leaders and fly anglers blind to hidden dangers and evolving threats.

Those filled with hubris become deluded by inflated self-evaluation,
over-estimate what can go right, under-estimate what can go
wrong, and are arrogant and contemptuous towards others' advice
and criticism. Hubristic leadership is fueled by prior successes and
praise, causing strengths to morph into weaknesses and bring out
unintended negative consequences. ~Eugene Sadler-Smith [20]

Founded in 1895, the Schwinn company became the dominant US bicycle maker by the middle of the 20th century. One in every four bicycles sold in the US was a Schwinn. And Schwinn's success came through constant product and production innovation.

Then, at the peak of its market share, Schwinn stopped peddling and began to coast. It lost focus on innovation and showed an unwillingness to invest in new manufacturing processes. For example, in the 1970s, West Coast entrepreneurs invented a whole new category of bikes, eventually called "mountain bikes," using modified Schwinn cruisers with European gearing. Schwinn's CEO, Edwin Schwinn Jr., dismissed the new advances made in automated factories as fads.

Gary Fisher, a cofounder of the Mountain Bikes company (now part of Trek), built his original models as Schwinn bicycle adaptations. When he approached the Schwinn company, its executives belittled him as an "amateur" and asserted: "*We know bikes.… We know better than anybody.*" Schwinn filed for bankruptcy in 1999.[21]

He who learns but does not think, is lost. He who thinks
but does not learn is in great danger. ~Confucius

Photo courtesy of Jack Murrey, Unsplash

Chapter 7
CONFIDENCE AND BELIEF

*Leaders and fly anglers have a strong belief that success is
just around the next corner, so they never give up.*
~Darrell Pardy

Chapter 7:
CONFIDENCE AND BELIEF

Perpetual optimism, believing in yourself, believing in your purpose, believing you will prevail, and demonstrating passion and confidence is a force multiplier. If you believe and have prepared your followers, they will believe and perform.
~General Colin Powell

One of the roles of a good guide is to instill confidence and belief in their clients. Confidence is magic, especially in fly fishing.
~Luciano Alba

Having confidence in a certain fly is vital for fly fishing. And here is where many guides make a big mistake. When guiding a client and approaching a section of water, they will often tell the client to fish the fly that the guide has confidence in. But does the client?

Professional guides learn to ask this question to their clients at the beginning of the trip. "What flies do you have the most confidence in? What are your go to flies?"

If the client has confidence in a certain fly and seems to be a reasonable choice for the water, they will be more confident and catch more fish. When the chips are down, let the client lead with what works for them. It can save an otherwise lost day.

~Bob Mallard

Most experienced fly fishers know there is something magical about a favorite fly pattern. It just seems always to catch fish, no matter what the situation. However, it's probably not a "killer" fly, but the way we fish it; with confidence, an intense focus and strong belief.

There's a lot of belief in fly fishing as well. Belief is knowing without seeing. Like knowing where the fish is, knowing how the fly works in the water to attract the fish, and knowing the moment before the fish takes the fly. ~Craig Langer

I believe in a concept called "my best self". If I have confidence in a specific technique or approach at work or on the river, my self-belief and capabilities are at their maximum, and I bring "my best self" to the task.

Three weeks ago, I was fly fishing, and conditions were tough. No hatch, no rises, no fish showing, dirty water, and wind making sight fishing impossible. I can nymph, but it's not an approach I have confidence with. I needed to bring my best self to this challenge.

I have great confidence, belief, and skill in my dry fly fishing capabilities, so in spite of the conditions, I put on a Royal Wolff and immediately took a very large Rainbow trout.

~Sean Monahan

Strong belief has a profound and visible effect on how an individual fishes a run or a pool. They are more attentive, mentally seeing the fly moving through the water, literally feeling the pulsation of a well-fished fly as it moves into the area where fish are holding. A confident fly angler feels "connected" to the fly and can sense any sudden stop or tug, almost before it happens. Belief and confidence give the fly angler a unique "sixth sense" that often results in many fish being landed.

*I usually go to the river carrying 50-100 flies of various
types, but I wind up fishing just 10% of them, mainly
because I know exactly how they fish, and I have confidence
in my ability to fish them properly. ~Bob Mallard*

I regularly fish for salmon in the Scottish Highlands and stay at the Oykel Bridge Hotel, just near the division between the Upper and Lower Oykel River beats. One evening I encountered a hapless fisherman at the hotel bar. The poor man had been fishing for two full days without a tug, let alone a fish landed. And he tried nearly every fly in his box. The man was nursing his pint of beer with a long face when I approached him.

I started a conversation by asking the man how many fish he caught. He lifted his head and said, sadly, none. How about you? He asked back. Well, I caught five yesterday and six today. The man almost spilled his beer. What fly were you using, he eagerly asked? My "magic" fly, I replied. I tell you, this little beauty always catches fish, even when others were getting skunked.

I then explained to him in great detail how this unique fly swam through the water, pulsating like a wounded fish and attracting the attention of even the most reluctant salmon. I used my hands to show how the rod tip should move to activate the fly in the water. I could see the man soaking the visual images into his mind's eye, his hands beginning to instinctively follow along. At the end of my magic fly story, I reached into my pocket and ceremoniously gave the man one. I expect to hear some great stories tomorrow evening, I remarked as we broke away for dinner.

That next evening at the bar, the man excitedly called me over and couldn't wait to tell me about his day. He explained how he could visualize the fly in the water, how it landed perfectly after his cast, and sank into the current. And best of all, he had pictures on his iPhone of his three fish!

I often tell this story with great delight because that particular fly just happened to be the only fly I had in my pocket at the time, and just one of the many flies I regularly fish on the Oykel.

~John Green

Confidence and belief have an almost magical power to help people perform at their best. Without belief, leaders and fly anglers will rarely succeed.

Here's a dramatic and sad example of the power of self-belief. For many years Tiger Woods was the top golf pro in the world. Some of his shots astounded onlookers and pros alike, almost like he had magic clubs and seeing-eye golf balls with laser sights. He had the confidence and gait of a champion as he moved around the golf course.

Then came the public exposure and humiliation of his sex addiction and marriage troubles. Tiger Woods' confidence and belief in himself was shattered. His ranking fell from first to fiftieth in just two years. It took him 11 years to win another major tournament. He didn't lose his golf skills, but he certainly lost his Mojo!

An important aspect of leadership is the ability to instill confidence and belief. John Green's "magic fly" was an attempt to help a man gain confidence and self-belief in his fishing abilities.

Far too many buy into the allure that their success and failure is due to a particular fly pattern. Without question, the majority of the time, it is due to the confidence of the angler and how they fish it. ~Mac Brown

Besides transferring energy into the organization, an effective leader also transfers a strong positive belief in the company's purpose, mission, strategy, and products to employees and customers. Unless employees believe in the company, its management, products, and services, the organization will never reach its potential no matter how well funded. In many cases, it will either fail or be the target of a takeover.

A bankruptcy judge can fix your balance sheet, but he cannot fix your company. ~Gordon Bethune

When an effective leader transfers belief and confidence to their employees, performance nearly always takes a positive turn. When Gordon Bethune became CEO of Continental Airlines in 1994, the airline was facing its third bankruptcy in 10 years, and Gordon was the 10th CEO in 12 years. Continental employees were so disheartened with the string of bad leaders, cost-cutting, and angry passengers, they routinely removed their logo patches when entering the grocery store to avoid abuse from disgruntled shoppers. The prevailing belief among pilots, flight attendants, mechanics, reservation teams, and managers was that Continental, the proud bird with the golden tail, was in a fatal tailspin, and nothing could save it.

Gordon Bethune understood the once-loyal Continental customer base, especially business travelers, were still out there, just pissed off and flying other airlines, even if it meant a non-direct flight. He also realized that belief, that same belief that powered the Wright Brothers to keep trying, was needed at Continental.

He understood the cause for the current toxic culture and poor performance in a few short weeks as the new CEO. Senior managers kept micromanaging every decision and continuously cut costs, hoping to improve the balance sheet. Punitive customer service policies kept employees from treating the customer fairly, which further angered passengers and frequent fliers.

Gordon knew the airline industry was a people industry, and he needed to re-instill pride and belief in Continental's 40,000 employees. It would require leadership and courage to pull off a sustainable turnaround and win back customers. In just two years, Continental went from the bottom of the airline tables on customer satisfaction, on-time arrivals, lost luggage, and employee turnover, to being voted airline of the year against 300 competitors. It consistently ranked in the top 4 in all DoT airline customer service statistics and returned to profitability. The Continental share price increased from $3.30 to $50 in just four years.

Talk about leadership and courage. Gordon Bethune fired senior and middle managers who no longer believed in the company or its people. He put the customer, not EBITDA, at the heart of the business strategy. He told the truth to employees in meetings, not memos or tweets, about why he decided to close certain hubs. He established a set of non-negotiable behaviors about how Continental employees should treat customers and each other. He burned the inches thick rule book and told ticketing and gate agents to use their best judgment to help the customer.

And he instituted a monthly cash bonus for all employees when the DoT customer service targets were met or exceeded. And lastly, he showed that he loved the company, its people, and their customers, by showing up at employee training classes and interacting with customers on flights.

*It may sound trivial to some, but the more confidence
I gained in my fly fishing abilities, the more courage I
gained in all other areas of my life. ~Jen Ripple*

Starting an international business from scratch was pretty scary for me, a first-time entrepreneur. But I took a large dose of confidence and courage from my fly fishing life and applied it to my start-up. My go-to fly is a Woolly Bugger. I have confidence in this fly. I know how it swims, how it moves in the water, how deep to fish it, and how to swing it in the current. And I almost always catch fish.

And in my business life, I have confidence in my selling skills. I know how customers think and how they react to new ideas. I understand the sales cycle and how to move from prospecting to an order. So,

I started my company based on a great idea, solid sales skills and processes, and excellent customer service.

~Ben Wright

Whenever I am on a new river, I tend to tie on what I call my "explorer" or "go to" fly, either an Elk Hair Caddis or a Parachute Adams. I have great confidence in these two flies, and I fish them with confidence as well. ~Graham Ellis

Wellness is not only a physical state, but a mental state. I am a firm believer in the mental concept of mind over body. I have first-hand experience. When I was diagnosed with cancer and told that the treatments were not working as expected, I adopted a mind over body approach. I took mental leadership of my body. For example, during my battle with the disease, I developed a mantra: "I don't get up to give up!" I believed in this mantra so much that my family and friends began to believe it as well. Effective leadership in business is a state of mind as well. Effective leaders have a belief that is so powerful it flows through the organization and into the body of the business.

~Christian Bacasa

CHAPTER 7: Confidence and Belief

Chapter 8

PROBLEM SOLVING AND
YOUR LEADERSHIP FLYBOX

Fly fishing is problem solving in the pursuit of fish.
Leadership is problem solving in the pursuit of customers.

Chapter 8:

PROBLEM SOLVING AND YOUR LEADERSHIP FLYBOX

One of the joys of fly fishing is problem-solving. There is not one way. There are a hundred ways. And the best anglers are prepared to try all of them.
~Domenick Swentosky

Sometimes a problem is actually the solution. For example, Christian Bacasa and I were dry fly fishing on a river in Montana and not having much luck. We tried nymphs and streamers, but nothing. We went back to dry flies, which didn't work until one of my flies sank a few inches below the surface. Usually this is failure of flotant to keep my fly on the surface, but I began to catch fish. This was the solution as the fish were feeding just below the surface.

In my leadership role as COO of a growing company, I always try to use problems as a pool of information that contains the solution. We just have to work it out. There is always a solution, and sometimes it's just rearranging the problem a certain way.

~Josh Dees

After many years of consulting, coaching, and observing leaders as they go about developing and executing their business strategies, I am always amazed at how sparse and narrow is their **"leadership**

flybox." In most cases, leaders have come to rely on one or two approaches in nearly all situations. The only change seems to be the level of intensity and loudness during meetings.

When I ask leaders about their past successes and leadership style, most say they have one specific approach (some focused, others demanding, or coaching, or intense pushing) that works for them. They tell me how well their leadership style worked in previous companies. Many often end the discussion with, "It's the way I get results."

When I ask: "Does it work in every situation?" Their reply is typical: "No, but you see the real problem is, people don't understand or just aren't capable, and they need to be replaced."

Really? Sounds to me like a myopic and lazy fisherman who refuses to change their approach and just keeps flogging the water with their favorite "go to" fly.

I was guiding a young man on the Henry's Fork. He was a keen and determined fly angler and excited about fishing this legendary river, known to be one of the toughest to fish, but having many large Brown and Rainbow trout, including the Cuttbow, a Cutthroat – Rainbow hybrid.

We fished all morning, and from the beginning, the young man struggled to get his casting rhythm with the light dry flies we were using, which is the typical way to fish this river. He kept at it, but with every cast, his confidence decreased. Seeing that he was mentally and physically worn out, I called for a lunch break.

He didn't say much during lunch, so I decided to ask what was the experience that got him hooked on fly fishing. I was hoping to improve his spirits before the next bout on the river. He told me he was raised in Texas, and in his first fishing experience, he threw a plastic frog into a pond and landed a 10lb bass. I could see his eyes light up as he recalled the incident.

That was the insight I needed. All morning we had been throwing light dry flies, and he was more used to streamer fishing. That afternoon we changed to streamers, something that is hardly ever done on this river. Immediately his shoulders squared up, he cast tight loops and hooked and landed several good-sized fish. Towards the end of the day, he landed one of the biggest trout I have ever seen on the Henry's Fork.

That experience taught me a valuable lesson about not always sticking with tradition, but trying new things that fit the client, not the guide. Our fly box is full of various flies, and we shouldn't be afraid to use them.

~Derek Hutton

Take at least five short casts before you cast far out into the middle of the river. Not all fish are 50 ft away. ~Heather Hodson

I got into fly fishing by accident. I was an IT professional and owned a growing technology development and service company. I enjoyed the world of technology because it matched my analytical nature and love of solving complex problems.

One weekend our company organized a corporate fly fishing retreat. Immediately I discovered how fly fishing fits my problem-solving and analytical nature, and it was outdoors! Plus, there was immediate feedback with every cast. From that day, I started studying everything

I could about fly fishing; the entomology, physics of casting, fly tying. Fly fishing is a thinking person's game.

~*Richard Fieldhouse*

Fly fishing is a great puzzle; it's about problem-solving. Every day you wake up, and the puzzle pieces are splayed out differently. No matter what tips or tricks you've figured out, there's always something new waiting around the next bend. ~Kirk Deeter [22]

Leaders are confronted with problems, but how they arrive at a decision tends to separate the real leader from those in title only. With a big, hairy complex problem, like fighting Al Queda terrorists in Afghanistan or orchestrating a merger and integration with another company, it's critical to tease out all the elements that interact with each other, rather than trying to develop a solution all at once.

Solving complex problems in business is the same as in fly fishing. You won't be successful in solving the entire problem at once, mainly because complex issues have hundreds of interconnected variables. Fly fishing is an interconnected ecosystem; current, structure, water temperature, water clarity, wind, time of day, cloud cover, etc. Complex business problems are a collection of interconnected variables.

As a young engineering executive, I learned a technique attributed to Ross Perot, the founder of Electronic Data Systems, an American multinational technology company. The approach was called "Dragon Slaying", where success depends upon starting at the beginning and fixing the little problems linked to other problems, which you then fix, and so on.

It's like pulling on the loose thread of a sweater and slowly unravelling the entire thing, stitch by stitch. Eventually, you wind up slaying the dragon (aka solving the problem).

~*Bob Mallard*

When one business leader discovered a label malfunction on a shipment of product going to a first time customer, with the possibility of an even larger future order, instead of panicking and just fixing the immediate issue, the senior team took a problem-solving approach. They quickly discovered the root cause and involved all related parties in the supply chain (label manufacturer, material suppliers, shipping and logistics, labeling machine operators, and even the customer). Not only did they fix the label problem and win the larger order, but they also discovered several weak steps in the entire value chain prone to errors and problems. The result was an overall improvement in quality, speed, and profitability.

A wind knot is usually a tiny knot, sometimes difficult to see, in your leader or tippet. Being so small, it looks harmless, and too many times, inexperienced anglers continue to fish rather than take the time to untie it and test the leader's strength before casting again.

Since the fishing gods like to play tricks on us flawed humans, invariably, the next cast with a wind knot is a hook up with a trophy fish, only to have the leader or tippet break off at the point of the wind knot under the strain.

And the same is true in business and life for that matter. Ignoring the little problems can be a recipe for disaster. Maybe not immediately, but at some point, that small problem links to an even bigger problem, which will be much harder to untangle. My advice in fly fishing and business is to deal with every little problem with the same care and urgency as if they were a huge issue, because left unresolved, they soon will be.

~*Joe Dilschneider*

You gotta know when to hold 'em,
Know when to fold 'em.
Know when to walk away,
Know when to run! ~*Kenny Rogers*

Much of success in fly fishing and leadership is about knowing when to push and when to wait. I was fishing in a spot where I knew a big trout should be holding. So instead of casting and casting in hopes that the fish was there, I just waited and watched, and finally, he moved. Now I had a real target to shoot for rather than a hoped-for one.

And the same is true for me in meetings. The leader should wait and let that uncomfortable silence hang in the air for a while. And most times, the client or others in the meeting will start to talk about their real issues. That moment of silence develops into an opportunity to address the underlying problems and work towards a sustainable solution. In both fly fishing and business, I call this the "pause that reveals."

~*Richard Commodore*

When a situation at work, or on the battlefield, gets confusing and uncertain, rather than pushing forward with the original strategy or planned approach, good leaders will call for a "Tactical Pause." A tactical pause is essentially a time out to gather new information and rethink the plan. With the business world moving faster than ever, good leaders will quickly assemble their leadership team and subject matter experts to reassess and refresh their strategy and execution plans.

In the military we learn to "go slow to go fast." Leaders, in most crises, can make better decisions by taking a deliberate pause, to assess what has gone right, what has gone wrong, and choose a better path forward. The financial markets did this in 2012 by implementing automatic halts to the markets if they drop 7 percent, 13 percent and 20 percent from the prior day's close. This is an automated way to allow traders to stop and reconsider why the markets are in free fall and prevent momentum from losing control. This gives the market makers and traders time to take a tactical pause and then make better decisions.

Organizations, left to their own devices, will not typically take the time to do so. Tactical pauses need to be institutionalized at every level of the organization. Senior leaders, as well as front line leaders, can benefit by doing so with their teams.

~Lieutenant General (Retired) Frank Kearney [23]

Several decades ago, Paul Hershey and Ken Blanchard came up with the concept of "Situational Leadership",[24] where leaders first determine the situation and the context they are facing, and then adjust their leadership behavior and approach to match the situation. A crisis may require a more collaborative, engaging leadership style. A changing competitive landscape or a sudden shift in technology might require a leadership style that encourages innovative ideas, risk-taking, and new ways of doing things. A merger or integration may require vision, diplomacy, and negotiation skills.

"Effective leaders need to be flexible and must adapt themselves according to the situation." ~Paul Hersey and Kenneth Blanchard

The Situational Leadership model has its drawbacks and is often seen as overly simplistic. However, the concept, when put into practice intelligently, has great merit. Instead of **matching the hatch**, leaders are **matching the situation** and the needs of people.

I've spent a lifetime in business developing others to take on leadership roles. And my fly fishing experiences have helped me craft a successful approach to leadership development.

The first job is to identify those individuals with potential. Something in their character and drive makes them stand out from others and fit well with the industry or the job function. The same is true for choosing the right fly and the right spot on the river to fish. There are lots of great flies, but the one that will catch fish is best matched for the circumstances.

Second, I sponsor them into jobs, roles, and situations that will cause them to stretch their capabilities. Challenging situations that require them to overcome a difficulty or confront their own lack of knowledge or skills. People learn more and develop confidence by stepping up and stepping into difficult situations. The same is true for becoming a better fly angler. We only improve our skills when fishing is the hardest.

Third, I put them into a role where they have to manage people as well as the business. I call it "becoming a factory manager" first, before you can become the leader. They must learn to balance both people skills and business skills to be successful. And improving in fly fishing is the same. You must balance an understanding of the fish, the river, your equipment, and yourself.

~Clement Booth

If the only tool you have is a hammer,
every job looks like a nail!

Next time you face a leadership challenge, take a moment to "stop, look, listen, and learn" before jumping into leadership autopilot mode. You might find that changing your approach produces better results all around. Every business situation is different, every stream is different. Don't approach either out of habit, but with thoughtful assessment.

"It's the client's goal that I must focus on, and that should stay
constant. My plans and approaches will change depending
upon the circumstances of the day. ~Capt. Skip Zink

In the artillery we hit our target through successive aims; some high, some low, some near and some far, until we can zero in every time.

Fly fishing is much the same. Successively changing flies, leaders, casts and mends to learn how the fish respond. And leadership with people takes time and different approaches to get it right.

~Don C. Puckett

My attitude about fly fishing is a lot like I live my life.
No matter what the conditions, I'm going, and my task
is to find a way to fish, period. ~Rick Porcello

The measure of success is not whether you have a
tough problem to deal with, but whether it is the same
problem you had last year. ~John Foster Dulles

I want someone new to the sport to start wherever they feel comfortable. I ask, "What is the smallest thing you can accomplish that will make you smile and feel more confident? Then let's start there." It's different for everyone. Maybe it's learning to tie a clinch knot or a loop knot. Maybe it's just casting on the lawn. The secret to entering a new sport, or solving a complex problem in business, is to break it down into small accomplishments that build on each other. Before long, you gain the skills and confidence that will keep you going.

~Tana Hoffman

Experience isn't the best teacher; it is the only teacher. ~Albert Schweitzer

Today, more than ever before, leaders of commercial, government, and non-governmental organizations are facing profound change that cuts across all industries, sectors, and national boundaries. The COViD-19 global pandemic has disrupted business strategies and human livelihoods everywhere. Creative problem solving is the most crucial capability our leaders can possess.

There is one constant about fly fishing; the conditions are never perfect. The fish aren't always rising, and the weather doesn't always cooperate. Maybe we get one perfect day in a lifetime of fishing. And it's that way in business. There is no perfect strategy, and every customer seems to want something slightly different.

That's why when I fly fish, I carry flies, lines, and equipment for most common eventualities. And I have learned multiple casting techniques to take advantage of whatever the weather and conditions are. And that same practice, of having a "diverse toolkit" in fly fishing,

I have used in my business career. Every time I have taken on a new role, I immediately decide what skills and knowledge I need in my "leadership toolkit" to be successful, and then I set about learning what is required.

~Tucker Horne

As a critical care nurse, I found that fly fishing helped improve my listening skills to understand my patients' deeper concerns. When you are night fishing for trout, you have to rely on your sense of hearing. When you are in a critical situation with an ill patient, listening to their breathing and other key indicators is vital.

Fly fishing has also taught me not to assume that I understand how to fish a river, even if I fished it yesterday. Instead, I need to quickly assess the current situation, such as weather, river conditions, time of day, hatches, and all the other things that impact fishing tactics. The same is true in nursing. I cannot assume the patient is the same as they were yesterday as their condition changes continuously. I need to quickly assess key conditions, like Airway, Breathing, and Circulation, to best deal with the patient.

~Heather Hodson

Chapter 9

GUIDES, MENTORS AND TRUST

It's important to get people on the water the right way. Fly fishing is not just about trophy photos and catch of the day, but more about the adventure and the journey. It is truly life changing.
~Dave Engen

"Education's purpose is to replace an empty mind with an open one."
~Malcolm Forbes

Chapter 9:

GUIDES, MENTORS AND TRUST

"The guide's job isn't to make fishing easy. It's to reveal the intricacies of a fluid puzzle; to evoke an appreciation for the relationship we share with our natural world; to lead the way."
~Will Benson

"We make a living by what we get, we make a life by what we give."
~Winston Churchill

My uncle Dan is the best fly angler I have ever met and also my mentor. I can ask him anything, and he knows how to accomplish it, with minimum effort. His mentoring is very effective.

He is very patient and watches me as I fish. Then he simply asks if he can share with me 2 or 3 things that might help me improve. And he waits for my reply, knowing that I'm the one doing the learning. Then he shows me a couple of things, watches while I use what he showed me, and then comes the important part. After a few tries we stop and he asks what I learned, how that felt, and what I could do to improve? It's interactive mentoring, not a one-way monologue.

~John Smigaj

How do people improve their skills and capabilities? How do they keep from plateauing in their career?

There are two schools of thought about personal and professional development. The classical view is that you first acquire knowledge and skills, practice, and keep learning until you get certified or graduate. Then you go out in the world and make your way, using the prior skills you have learned. The problem with this approach is that it is almost impossible to see your blind spots, which keep you from recognizing issues within yourself that get in the way of continuous improvement.

What would you tell a beginner that would open up the doors on fly fishing? Don't overthink it. Enjoy what you're doing at the moment. Don't think about what you should have done or how your day should have gone. Don't worry so much about fly patterns. Practice casting, no matter what you do. It's hard for fly angler's not to overthink because it's a thinking person's pursuit. But observe what's going on and pay attention to what's happening instead of what you think should happen.

~Tom Rosenbauer [25]

*My advice to a young executive keen to move into the leadership ranks is to **make decisions**. Take the decision, take accountability for the outcome, learn all you can from that experience, then make more decisions. And be willing to change your decision based on new information. ~Gordon Sim*

All leaders need mentors, and all leaders should serve as mentors to others as well. ~Todd Degrosseilliers

The second school of thought about development comes from sports. In sports, everyone has a coach. Everyone needs a coach. Good coaches are your external eyes and ears, providing a more accurate picture of your performance. They see the fundamentals that you may have missed and bad habits you have developed as a workaround.

Mel Kreiger, one of the most famous fly fishing teachers of my generation, came to Sweden with his wife, Fanny, and invited me to join them on a fly fishing trip to the famous trout rivers of the Jämtland area. I met him briefly years ago at a fly fishing fair and recall mentioning how much I enjoyed his book, *The Essence of Fly Casting*. Needless to say, I didn't know what to expect from such a famous person, nor how I should act. I expected my role to be the "local expert" and act as an unofficial guide. I expected to blend into the background.

Well, that wasn't what happened. From the moment we met, Mel began to share with me, a relative stranger, his knowledge and love of casting, fishing, and life. Not only was Mel a great fly caster and fisherman, but an outstanding people person. He got great joy from sharing his knowledge with others. When Mel was fishing that week, he gave me tips, lessons, and nuggets of information.

That experience taught me an important lesson about leadership and success. In both business and fly fishing, the essence of a successful career is about giving and helping others learn and improve. As a result, I spent a large part of my time organizing fly fishing events and conferences in both Sweden and around the world during my career. I realized that giving to others made me much happier in the long run than just catching lots of fish.

~Harry Salmgren

A good guide or casting instructor is essential for those keen to learn and improve. And for those who aspire to leadership roles, it's not only important to have a mentor, but also to be a good mentor for others.

Leaders require mentors in the same way that a fly angler requires a guide. Guides show us the way to find success in fly fishing. Our mentors show us the way to successful leadership. A great leader plans for succession and actively develops ethical leadership in others. Similarly, a great fly angler takes the time to teach others to learn the sport, care for the environment, and respect each other. Both make the world a better place for future generations.

~Todd Degrosseilliers

A mentor can provide motivation and advice on everything from where to park your truck to what type of wading boots to buy, to how to set the hook. But it is not just about the right advice, it is about the right advice FOR YOU. Everyone is different. A mentor is valuable because they know you, and they know what you need to know. ~Jason Shemchuk

I grew up fly fishing with my father in the Lake Tahoe area. As a young kid, I was free to jump on my bike, grab my hand-me-down fly rod and head off to the river in a pair of tennis shoes and shorts. I learned to tie a few flies at my father's bench, and that's what I fished with most of my young adult life. I wasn't a sophisticated fly angler. I approached it more like street basketball, having fun mattered more than style or skill.

One day a client invited me on a fly fishing trip. I never fished with a guide before. I was blown away by his professionalism and thoughtfulness about the river, the fish, and the environment. I learned the subtleties of fly fishing from him. That encounter changed my whole approach to the sport. I'm not a gearhead or fashion maven, but I am more equipped for many fishing challenges on the river. He even taught me the "bow and arrow" cast, which I would never have picked up independently. Since that day, I've had a new respect for guides and mentors. A good guide, or business mentor can shortcut the path to success, and I'm all for that.

~Justin Fortier

It's not how good you are now, but how good you could be that matters. ~Dr. Atul Gawande, Surgeon

What constitutes a "good" business mentor or a "good" guide? I believe the foundation of an effective mentor and fly fishing guide is a unique blend of capability, tact, and brutal honesty. Tact keeps the ears of the mentee or client open and receptive, and brutal honesty quickly gets to the heart of the issue. Too often, mentors and guides are reluctant to upset their clients, which leads to watered-down coaching and a lack of real improvement.

I was leading a corporate fly fishing retreat with a very dominant CEO and about 15 of his key executives. Everyone was excited to learn more about fly fishing, catch a few large trout, and generally bond with each other. In these events, part of the learning is about fly fishing, and the other is what they learn from each other about work and life.

Everyone was excited, but none more so than the CEO, who was obviously used to being in charge and the center of attention. I was informed before the event that he was somewhat of a bully and very domineering at the office, and his behavior in the first 30 minutes showed me that was an understatement. He was running around, advising all of his team as they were learning the fundamentals of casting. And in a not so nice way. In fact, the day's tone was rapidly turning sour, and a few of the executives began complaining behind his back to each other.

It became pretty obvious something had to change. As the leader and senior guide on this outing, it was up to me. Fly fishing is all about feedback, both from the casting quality and the human interactions.

So, I took him aside and told him that he needed to back off. Not only so his team could learn on their own and feel good about their progress, but for health and safety reasons as well. Already he had several near misses from backcasts as he was running around giving "advice."

He stopped, went silent, turned, and walked off. About 10 minutes later, he came back and thanked me. "You know, I rarely get good, honest, straight feedback. And I do want my team to learn and have a great conference. You are right. I was getting in the way. I do that at work as well."

All in all, it turned out to be a great corporate retreat, and several executives thanked me for "helping" the boss!

~Ben Bangham

One of the characteristics of a good guide is courage! And the same is true for a business coach or mentor. Courage to step up and step into an issue that is not working or deteriorating quickly. Not everyone wants to hear the truth, but everyone needs the truth, especially if they're going to improve themselves, their skills, their employees, and their organization.

Like in the story above, the best approach is to affirm the goal the person is after. Is it farther casts, more fish, less effort, reading the water? Is it a better management team, more innovation, more productive meetings? Then help the person see a blind spot keeping them from their goal. And don't beat around the bush. Just as a weak, sloppy cast catches few fish, watered-down feedback does little good.

*Criticism may not be agreeable, but it is necessary. It fulfills
the same function as pain in the human body. It calls attention
to an unhealthy state of things. ~Winston Churchill*

Not all those in a leadership role are good leaders. But the turn from mediocre to outstanding leader can come quickly after a healthy dose of honest feedback.

*Failures are the guide's responsibility. If the client fails,
you failed. That sounds harsh, but it is the mindset that
will push you to be a better guide. ~Tom Sadler*

I facilitated a senior leadership retreat for a large US defense manufacturer when the time came for practicing feedback. Everyone in the room agreed feedback was important for improving new products or new business processes, improving team dynamics, and personal effectiveness.

To illustrate a useful tool for giving appreciative and constructive feedback, I chose the senior program manager for their largest military contract to practice this technique with me in front of the class. This individual was an MIT graduate engineer, a brain the size of a planet, stood six foot three inches tall, and had been the vocal critic during the entire three-day workshop.

I said, *"Dick, what I appreciate about you is your willingness to speak your mind and to bring up different points of view for us to consider."* He puffed up and replied with a loud, *"Thank you."* I continued with the other half, constructive feedback. It went like this. *"Dick, I think you could be even more effective if you weren't such a bully and kept putting people down for their ideas. You may not realize this, but when you walk down the hall, you leave dead bodies in your wake! Listening to ideas from others is a good way for everyone to learn together."*

He nearly exploded and adamantly denied any such behavior and sat down. The workshop ended with much progress, but the event with Dick didn't end there.

A month later, I conducted a follow-up day with the team to discuss the projects and improvements they agreed in the last workshop. Right after I said good morning to the group, Dick raised his hand and asked to speak. *"I couldn't believe the feedback I got, not only from you, but from every member of the team over this past month. I never realized how my behavior impacted others. My wife even chimed in! I get it now. Thank you everyone."*

Several years later, I was invited back to the same company, and Dick was now the CEO. He turned out to be an outstanding leader of the business and people, and later in his career, was tapped to turn around a troubled defense company.

> *Most of the time, when dealing with a jerk client or a brash young MBA, if you work to make them successful, they will realize how little they know and will move from jerk mode to learner mode. That is real leadership.* ~Tom Sadler

Fly fishing, like any sport, is difficult to learn on your own. Most of us don't have enough fishing time to practice everything required to become even remotely competent. And then there is knowledge about rivers and fish to learn. Fortunately, there are many excellent blogs and videos to impart knowledge on just about everything related to fly fishing. But watching a video doesn't develop skills and that all-important fishing instinct. That's where a good guide and mentor comes in. They will save us a great deal of time and help us avoid numerous mistakes.

I owned commercial and residential real estate firms for many years before retiring and becoming a fly fishing guide. In my real estate companies, I had many employees and agents, and my job as the leader was to figure out how to grow the company and make it profitable. I soon figured out that the key was to make my staff successful. Through various individual conversations and staff meetings, I let them know that the company could only be a success if they were successful at their jobs, and my role was to figure out a way to make each of them a success. Sometimes that meant giving advice or changing things inside the company that inhibited or blocked their success.

And the same is true in my guide business. I see my job as figuring out how to make each client successful, based on their goals and motivations for the trip. And since every client is different, I listen and observe their personality styles from the moment we meet. This approach gives me early clues as to their motivations and expectations for our fishing day.

~Capt. Skip Zinc

However, not all guides are effective in dealing with clients.

After spending a rainy week with several different guides on Cape Cod fishing for Striped Bass, I couldn't help but notice how the individual guides' personality and communication style impacted not only the fishing experience but the fishing itself. And the more I watched, the more I began to see a recurring pattern. I have classified their styles as either **Projectors** or **Receptors**.

To get a visual of what I mean by a "Projector" personality, think of a large movie projector that is constantly running, reel after reel after reel. It rolls on and on continuously. There doesn't seem to be an "off" switch in sight! Not only is it noisy (notice how most movie theatres have the sound cranked way up?), but it creates a lot of heat. And that heat is transferable to others. When molecules and people get hot, they get agitated. Got the picture (and the analogy)?

A guide with a "projector personality" seems to be always talking but rarely listening. It seems their ears shrink, and the excess energy moves over to the mouth. Not only don't they listen, but they also don't seem interested in understanding the client's particular expectations and desires. They have their set pitch, their set pattern of where to fish, how to fish, and how long to fish. Like a continuous loop projector, they keep saying the same things over and over, going to the same spots over and over, and using the same techniques, over and over.

And they don't like it when a client tries to break the pattern. *"The fish won't go for that fly. That technique won't work. Here, use one of my rods, it's rigged up properly."*

During our Striped Bass fishing, the days seemed to get longer and longer with this type of guide. We were only saved by the fact that the fishing was fabulous. We soon learned to tune out the noise and the endless chatter in the background.

Contrast that with the guide with a "receptor personality". To get an image of a receptor, think of a caricature of a person with giant ears and a small mouth, much like a long-eared hare.

The "receptor" guide asked open-ended questions and listened intently, understanding each of his clients' unique idiosyncrasies. One was a left-hand caster, the other right-hand. One had fished saltwater extensively, the other sporadically. Both were new to Cape Cod. On and on the questions came, not aggressively or excessive, but measured, as one would play a large fish. After listening to our desires, concerns, and expectations, he built a game plan around us. We fished two days in solid rain and wind with a "receptor personality" guide and had an excellent time. Even the wind seemed manageable as he worked with us to learn heavy wind casting techniques. And I dare say he was enjoying himself as well.

At the end of the trip, our fishing group ranked the guides. To a person, the "projector" came out on the bottom and the "receptor" on top, no matter what the fishing conditions.

A guide may cast like Lefty Kreh, and know the water and the fish like a native, but how well do they understand their behavior and its impact on the fishing experience?

I can't help but reflect on the fact that these two behavior types show up in the executive boardroom and on senior management teams as well. And the experience for their employees is the same.

The good Lord gave us two ears and one mouth
and expects us to use them in that proportion!
~a phrase I heard regularly from my mother

The best mentors in my fly fishing life were people I met on the river.
Those who take fly fishing seriously are generally good people. And
in the leadership class I teach at UCLA, I use a book titled, **Good**
People. *All leadership starts and ends with people. ~Fred Owusu*

Our Reel Recovery retreats are staffed with volunteers, many of whom pair up with a cancer patient to be their buddy during the retreat. The buddies serve as "broad shoulders" for wading, helping with tying on flies and other fly fishing assistance, but mostly caring listeners. It's when cancer patients can talk openly with someone who listens and cares that the emotional healing begins.

We've had hundreds of volunteers over the past 17 years, and everyone has openly said that being a buddy to a cancer patient during the retreats probably helped them as much, or more than the other way around. It fills their heart to be of service and renews their spirit, much more than any trophy fish they ever caught.

~Stan Golub

Trust is the glue of life. It's the most essential ingredient
in effective communication. It's the foundational principle
that holds all relationships. – Stephen M. R. Covey

The more they trust you, the more they'll learn. ~Dan Michels

Our fly fishing lodge draws numerous industry leaders and politicians every year, all seeking an opportunity to get out into the real Alaskan bush, away from their endless round of meetings and decisions. It's akin to a mental health break for many of them. However, the Alaskan weather and fishing conditions don't always match their expectations for a once a year get-away holiday.

Being unable to control the situation is often difficult for most senior executives. They want to fly out and get fishing, but if the weather closes in, we can't fly. It is evident from their remarks and behavior that they are agitated, frustrated, and even angry at not being in control.

This is where trust comes into play. We spend time, from the moment guests first arrive at the lodge, building trust. To us, trust is the foundation for a successful Alaskan fly fishing and outdoor experience. Without trust, we couldn't keep our clients safe, since many of the rules for safety on the water and in the bush are alien to them. Without trust, we couldn't turn a washout fishing day into a life-long learning experience through educating them about fish behavior and fly fishing, the delicate ecological balance of the wilderness, and about the vital importance of conservation and sustainability. Strong trust speeds up the learning process and heightens the experience.

~*Dan Michels*

Trust is the currency of effective leadership. Command and control leadership is fading fast, and in all honesty, it never was that effective in the first place. It's not long before people stop trying, productivity declines, innovation grounds to a halt, and the leader is replaced. With trust, leaders encourage people to do things they never thought they could do, to take on challenges that stretch and grow their skills and confidence. Trust allows us to take that leap of faith that produces amazing results.

On the sea, there is a tradition that with responsibility goes
authority and accountability. Men will not long trust leaders
who feel themselves beyond accountability for what they do. And
when men lose confidence and trust in those who lead, order
disintegrates into chaos and purposeful ships into uncontrollable
derelicts. ~Wall Street Journal – Editorial 14 May 1952

And guides can learn from their clients as well.

I remember joining a company as a new middle manager, and it came time for the traditional company banquet and auction. A raffle was set up and people were auctioning off cooking ware, garden equipment, and the likes. I decided to offer up a guided fly fishing day, with me as the guide. I thought it would be an excellent way to meet people in the company.

When the bidding started, I could see that the CEO was keen to win the trip, but he was constantly outbid by a consultant working for the company. I wanted the CEO to win as it would be great to spend an entire day with the CEO. Good for my learning, and maybe even my career.

The bidding kept going back and forth, and eventually, the consultant won. I was disappointed and mentally decided this guy was my sworn enemy. However, the consultant could cast and fly fish, and he turned into my business mentor and, over the years, an excellent friend. It's been a dozen years since that raffle, and I have learned a great deal about leadership, business, and life from my friendship with him. Actually, he helped me more in my career advancement than a day fishing with the CEO could have.

~Brian Wetter

If you take a grain of wheat and make a loaf of bread, the value add is three times. If you take a rough diamond and polish it, a good diamond cutter creates ten to fifteen times its value. However, if you take a human being, mentor, and nurture him or her, the value add is infinite. ~Jadish Sheth

A good Board of Directors and a good guide are very similar. They should remain impartial and give honest and direct assessments and advice. But the choice is always yours. ~Clement Booth

CHAPTER 9: Guides, Mentors and Trust

Photo courtesy of Samantha Deleo, Unsplash

Chapter 10

SHADOW OF THE LEADER

The number one thing that holds fly anglers back from catching a lot more trout is an aversion to changing their leaders. There are very few situations where one leader setup does the trick all day long. And a (good) do-it-all style of leader doesn't really exist. Taking the middle of the road approach leaves you average at both ends.

~Domenick Swentosky

Chapter 10:

SHADOW OF THE LEADER

Organizations are shadows of their leaders;
that's the good news and the bad news.

One day, I guided a very keen angler on a highly productive river, but the fishing was awful. I suggested changing flies, which we repeatedly did, but no luck. Now I know this particular river, and there is a lot of fish, and some good-sized ones. Even though he was a competent angler, still no fish.

So, I suggested the problem may be in the leader, particularly its length. The fish were rising but not taking our fly. I lengthened the leader as I felt the fly line landing on the water may have caused a slight disturbance making the trout warier. Adding extra leader meant the distance between fly and fly line is greater and therefore provides less chance of spooking the fish. He hooked up immediately and had excellent fishing for the rest of the day.

As I thought about this later, it occurred to me that lengthening the fly fishing leader is a lot like a business leader spending additional time with an employee who is having a hard time being successful at their job. I have often experienced bosses who are short and sharp with their communications and requests, whereas taking the extra time for a longer, more accurate conversation can make all the difference to that employee's confidence and performance.

~Pete Tyjas

Choosing the right fly fishing leader takes considerable thought since the wrong sized leader can spook the fish as it lands or cast a shadow in the water. And the correct length of leader is also important in getting the fly to swim properly and reach the zone where the fish are holding.

I'd personally rather fish the wrong fly on the right leader than the other way around. ~Louis Cahill [26]

With the wrong leader set up, you might as well be casting in your yard. And the same is true in business. With the wrong leader it's hard to deliver a quality product or service. ~Fred Owusu

Choosing the right leader in business is critical. Shortly after Alan Mulally became CEO of Ford Motor Company in 2006, instead of responding to an email in kind, which was standard Ford practice, he would walk into the person's office or call them, even lower-level employees. Stories circulated about the new boss and his open communication style and his real interest in listening to ideas. Mulally's behavior was inspiring and up-lifting. Through individual acts of reaching out and connecting with people, he built up a tired and insecure organization's morale. Mulally became the unofficial Chief Engagement Officer, and employees responded to his openness, optimism and direct style.

Leaders either catch fish or spook them.
Leaders either grow people or suppress them.

What is your leadership shadow? Those in leadership positions cast shadows far and wide across their company.

Whether you know it or not, **YOU** cast a powerful shadow in your organization through your everyday actions. And actions speak louder than words! People watch the behavior of their leaders for clues as to what is accepted and what is not. When a leader says one thing and then behaves differently, employees quickly figure out the real story. One of the major obligations of leadership is integrity between words and deeds!

When you come into the building and head straight for your office, head down, not interacting with anyone, that's the story that gets talked about in the canteen and the pubs, not the speech you gave on employee engagement and openness.

> *A leader doesn't just get the message across, a*
> *leader is the message! ~Dr. Warren Bennis*

The senior team and how they interact with each other casts another powerful shadow. If you want teamwork as a core value across the organization, it must happen at the top, or you won't achieve it anywhere in the company, even with the best team building workshops.

If two senior executives don't support each other, you can forget about support and cooperation between departments. This type of poor leadership shadow led to the nuclear accident at Three Mile Island, and countless other examples of sub-optimal performance inside organizations.

Want to learn more about leadership shadows in your organization? Listen to the company jokes; look at the cartoons and pictures posted in cubicles; read the graffiti in the bathroom stalls; ask your suppliers; ask your customers; ask middle management. Look in the cultural mirror of your company – it's all there if you are willing to see it.

> *A fish rots from the head, first!*

As COO of a brewing company, when COVID-19 hit, I was on a conference call with peers discussing the biggest concerns for our businesses. Others mentioned many important business issues, such as disruption in the supply chain for materials, disruption in distribution to our customers, reduced business, and income loss.

When asked about my concerns and priorities, I shared what our CEO told me. He said your number one priority, above all else, is our employees' health and safety. Solve that first, then worry about the rest.

That statement, and the CEO's principles and values, cast a huge positive shadow over our entire management team, helped keep our people safe, and rallied us together as we work to keep our business safe and productive through the uncertainty that lies ahead.

~Sean Monahan

One of the most impactful shadows cast by leaders is whether they are fully engaged in strategy execution. Some say it's the role of the leader and senior team to define the strategy and for middle managers and employees to execute. In my experience, the handoff between senior and middle management is more like a dropped baton in a relay race.

There is no strategy without execution,
and there is no execution without leadership.

A research study by the management consulting firm Towers Perrin of over 400 companies found that 49% of the leaders reported a gap between their organization's ability to formulate a strategy and deliver results. Shockingly, only 36% of the leaders in companies with an execution gap had confidence in their organization's ability to close the gap! [27]

"I can get you to a fish, but the last 50 feet is up to you!" ~Capt. Skip Zink

On the other hand, there have also been some spectacular demonstrations of execution. How did Gordon Bethune and Greg Brenneman orchestrate the massive turnaround of Continental Airlines, with 40,000 employees, in one year (1994-1995) from being $2.5 billion in default and having 10 years of successive losses to a

$200+ million profit in 1995 and leading the global airline league tables for the next 10 years?

How did Alan Mulally, Lewis Booth, and the senior team of Ford Motor Company, without bailout money from the US government, engineer a massive turnaround in profitability, market share, and customer satisfaction?

How did Bill McLaughlin, a former senior executive from PepsiCo, take a failing Minneapolis-based mattress manufacturer, Sleep Comfort, and build it into an international business with high growth, excellent profits and raving customers? The answer is the ability to focus on relentless execution.

For me, leadership has many components, such as setting a clear vision, inspiring others, and adapting to the unexpected. But perhaps the most important of all is relentless execution. ~Paul Hoobyar

The leadership principle I've learned from fly fishing is what I call, **Trimming the Fat**, which is my way of saying stop overthinking and over designing, and just execute. I see a lot of fly anglers carrying too many flies and spending too much time strategizing about which fly to use. Sometimes so much so that they don't get their fly in the water enough during the day. The more your fly is in the water the higher probability of catching a fish. Execute, don't over think.

And I've seen the same pattern in my business career, where leaders spend more time on fancy PowerPoint presentations and analyzing data than on actual execution of their plans. Leading meetings rather than leading execution is a design to fail.

~John Smigaj

No matter how expensive your rod is and how big your fly box, you won't catch fish unless your fly is in the water.

Photo courtesy of ©Jay Beyer

Chapter 11
CULTURE MATTERS

Culture is simply a shared way of doing something with a passion
~Brian Chesky, Airbnb

Chapter 11:
CULTURE MATTERS

If you don't understand your culture,
you don't understand your business.

Somebody behind you, while you are fishing, is as bad as someone
looking over your shoulder while you write a letter to your girl.
~Ernest Hemingway.

All organizations, organized sports and associations, whether start-up or decades old, private or public, have a set of ground rules, usually unwritten but generally understood and followed by its members, that define what behaviors, actions, and beliefs are acceptable or not. It's known as their organizational culture, and every culture is unique. What is important about culture, especially in business organizations, is that it directly influences how people behave and has a direct impact on business results.

Culture is not neutral. It either strengthens or weakens the organization. A culture aligned with the company ethos, values, and strategy, and in which all members clearly understand and respect the ground rules, is considered strong and enables high performance. Those organizations where the ground rules are vague, leadership is disconnected, profit or image is more important than people or quality, tend to struggle.[28]

In some industries and institutions, such as global investment banking, cultures have been described as "toxic" and resulted in systemic fraud and massive fines. Between 2009 and 2019, global financial institutions were fined more than $360 billion for fraudulent practices resulting from casino-like corporate cultures.

Culture is the product of leadership combined with policies and practices that create and reinforce *"the way we do things around here"*.

Fly fishing, like business, is a long game and it's important for us to keep earning our customer's trust so they will spread the good word about our company. You can't become competent at fly fishing overnight, and you can't build a trusted and respected brand overnight. It's critical for individuals and a business to have a set of values that will support the long game.

Understanding that fly fishing is a long game helped me make a painful business decision, which in the long run was the right decision. We had just designed a new rod series and finally received the first shipment from our manufacturer. We were excited, until we noticed a small aesthetic discrepancy. It wasn't a problem with the rod's performance, but it was not the quality we wanted. It was a $100,000 plus decision. Do we scrap the shipment and start over, or go ahead, sell the rods and do better next time?

Fortunately, our company has a strong culture and a vision to be a world leader in the value-priced fly fishing rod market. We don't cut corners. We put the entire shipment in our warehouse and started over. For us, the long game is the only game to be playing.

~Tate Cunningham

Fly fishing, like any sport, has a strong and unique culture with a plethora of unwritten ground rules, specific vocabulary, specially designed clothes and equipment, and an ethos centered around sustainability and environmental stewardship.

At many lodges, the guides do their job, drop off the guests and head home to their families. That was the culture at our lodge, and guests noticed the distance between themselves and the guides. Our fishing was great, but our customer loyalty and return visits were not what we wanted.

After a few new younger guides joined us, they started a habit of sitting out back behind the kitchen after dinner and talking about, you guested it, the day's fishing, what they learned on the river that day, and how to best help their clients.

Some of the guests heard the laughter and started joining them after dinner. You could just feel a new culture grow, one of openness, inclusion, and a thirst for sharing and learning. My dad noticed this and decided we should build a large deck, complete with a fire pit and a fridge for beer.

The guides loved it, but so did the guests, and I believe our guests learn just as much from those evenings of stories and tips as they do fishing all day on the river. Our inclusive culture has become a huge selling point for our lodge.

~Wade Fellin

Culture is mostly about belonging to a group of people with similar beliefs, interests, and values. In these groups, traditions and rituals pass from expert to novice and from guides to clients. Fly fishing has numerous traditions, symbols, rituals, and unwritten ground rules, as does every sport, business, and organization. All have cultures, either by design or default. And culture has an ingrained acceptance and rejection mechanism, which helps maintain and strengthen group cohesion.

Out on the river, there is no color or division between people. We are all fly anglers looking out for the river, the fish, and each other. ~Richard Commodore

One of the things I like about fly fishing is that for many people, it is a cross-generational activity where values and life lessons can be passed from one generation to the next in a way that imbeds them deeply.

My parents divorced when I was young, and my mother and I spent a lot of time with my grandfather, a keen fly angler. He would take me fishing with him, partly to teach me the skills but also to help heal from the pain of my parent's splitting up. And he would talk to me, not just about fishing, but about life, life's ups and downs, and his own life experiences. Those days fishing with my grandfather left a deep and meaningful impression on me.

~Mark George

Strong cultures have healthy Norms, which are defined as beliefs and ways of behaving that are important for belonging and group cohesion. And fly fishing has numerous Norms, many of which are unwritten ground rules. To violate the fly fishing culture's Norms is to be branded as an outsider or avoided when others are organizing a fishing trip.

Here are a few of the fly fishing cultural norms:

- Obey laws and respect property rights and ask for permission to fish on private land,
- Littering is unacceptable. You are expected to take out more than you brought in,
- Avoid wading in spawning areas and wade carefully so as not to disturb the fish or the natural ecology of the river,

- Keep a reasonable distance from other anglers and move on if another angler is there first,
- Keep quiet and don't spoil the solitude, plus loud talking and shouting scares the fish as well as annoys other anglers,
- If a nearby angler needs help netting a fish, or is in trouble, offer assistance,
- Respect your guide and their instructions as they have your safety, well-being, and goals in mind
- Keep moving and don't stay in one place too long, let the fish rest and also let others have an opportunity
- Practice catch and release and use barbless hooks,
- Keep the fish wet when taking photos and return them quickly.

Understanding and obeying the Norms in fly fishing will lead to many memorable and enjoyable experiences.

> *Sometimes the first cast will be your best opportunity, so don't rush it and don't go ahead until you are completely ready. And in business, you don't get a second chance to make a first impression. ~Tate Cunningham*

Business, community, and political leaders who design and support their organization's specific culture to benefit multiple stakeholder groups create profitable and sustainable organizations. Those leaders who let culture evolve by default live with a set of Norms, behaviors, and results that are middle of the road, or worse.

> *I used to believe that culture was 'soft' and had little bearing on our bottom line. What I believe today is that our culture has everything to do with our bottom line, now and into the future. ~Vern Dosch*

Netflix designed their corporate culture from the start and even created what they call a "Culture Deck" used during the hiring and onboarding of new employees. Their overall vision: **To continue being one of the leading firms of the internet entertainment era,**[29] is supported and enabled by their innovation culture. And innovation means hiring for diversity, valuing new ideas, and then being willing to change based on market and consumer changes, which Netflix has done several times throughout its corporate history.

CHAPTER 11: Culture Matters

Over the years, we learned that if we asked people to rely
on logic and common sense instead of on formal policies,
most of the time we would get better results, and at a lower
cost. - Patty McCord, Chief Talent Officer, Netflix

When adding people into a company, especially in senior and middle management roles, many advisors often speak about "cultural fit." I got some excellent advice from one of my mentors. He said, "Forget about cultural fit unless you want a company of clones. You should be seeking out those who will be culturally additive"! As a result, we have built a solid, high-performance company. It's not only a place where I like to work, but our employees love working here.

~*Ben Wright*

High-performance cultures contain many Norms and values, but more often than not, one Norm, in particular, becomes the foundation, or platform, upon which continued success and sustainability is based. When David Novak took over as CEO of YUM! Brands, a collection of fast food companies (Pizza Hut, Kentucky Fried Chicken, and Taco Bell) in 1999, annual revenues were around $4 billion. David's objective was to grow the organization into a global company, but what kind of culture could tie such different brands together and power a global company with over 20,000 restaurants in multiple countries?

From his early days at an accounting firm and then as an executive at PepsiCo, David understood that recognition is a powerful force in people's lives. Positive recognition in the workplace inspires and motivates people at all levels. David started to build the YUM! Brands culture based first and foremost on individual and team recognition. Where other global restaurant chains focused on profit and costs, David realized that these essential elements of company success were the outcomes of a high-performance culture and inspired people.[30]

When Novak retired from YUM! Brands in 2016, the company had 41,000 restaurants globally and annual revenues of $32 billion. David Novak was recognized as CEO of the Year in 2012 by Chief Executive Magazine and one of the "100 Best-Performing CEOs in the World" by the Harvard Business Review.

Real leaders dare to make a positive difference in the world. And fly fishing is a wonderful vehicle to make a difference to people, society, and the environment. ~Margot Page

Leaders must take responsibility to build and maintain a safe environment and culture for their employees and be accountable for the consequences of their decisions. Just as a river guide must take responsibility for the complete safety and well-being of his clients. ~Paul Hoobyar

Photo courtesy of ©Angela Hemingway Charles

Chapter 12:

ENCOUNTERS THAT CHANGE YOU

When two people meet and exchange a dollar, both walk away
with a dollar. But when they exchange ideas, both are richer.
~Thomas Jefferson

Chapter 12:
ENCOUNTERS THAT CHANGE YOU

All my life, I feel like the river has guided me.
~Mark George

In everyone's life, at some time, our inner fire goes out. It is then burst into flame by an encounter with another human being. We should all be thankful for those people who rekindle the inner spirit.
~Albert Schweitzer

In the late summer of 2000, a good friend and outstanding fly angler, John Green, invited me to go fly fishing for Atlantic Salmon in Iceland. John and I fished together numerous times in Scotland, and I was looking forward to his company and fishing stories. On the plane from London, John informed me that we were staying at a lodge whose guests that week included Jack Hemingway and his wife, Angela, as well as Orri Vigfusson, the ardent and innovative wild salmon conservationist. It promised to be an exciting week, and it was my first time fishing the gin-clear water of Icelandic rivers.

While John Green was an accomplished Iceland salmon fisherman, this was my first experience with tiny flies and spooky fish in gin clear water. It took several days for me to get in the groove and hook and land a few of these massive, bright, formidable fighting creatures.

But Jack was a seasoned veteran of Iceland salmon fishing and was high-rod for most of the week. Jack Hemingway was never without a smile and a hearty laugh, and he never boasted about himself. It must have been difficult being the son of such a famous author and sportsman. Still, Jack was his own person, having a myriad of adventures as an OSS officer in WWII and a keen conservationist and sportsman.

At the dinner table each evening, we would hear stories that ranged from his famous father to his adventure of parachuting into occupied France with his fly rod, just in case, he came across a trout stream. Alas, he was captured and spent the remainder of the war in a German POW camp. Jack wrote two books, **Mis-Adventures of a Fly Fisherman** and **A Life Worth Living**, both about his life, family and fishing.

Sadly, Jack Hemingway passed away just a few months after our fishing trip. I'll bet he's still smiling and telling stories.

I think of that week with Jack Hemingway often. Not only because I was in the presence of real royalty, but also a great fly angler and human being. When those rare, few, and far between chance meetings happen while fly fishing, there are leadership lessons to be learned. The most potent lesson for me from fishing with Jack Hemingway was his gentle nature, his ability to laugh at anything, especially himself, and his steely focus and concentration when fishing.

As a young boy, my mother told me that the secret to talking to anyone was to be interested, not interesting. So, at a particularly fishy pool with Jack, I asked him the following question: *"What leadership lessons have you learned from your years of fly fishing?"*

He stopped and looked at me while tying on one of those small Salmon flies used in the Icelandic rivers. Even over the roar of the nearby falls, I could hear his mental wheels churning. There was a long pause, and when he spoke, I was taken entirely by surprise. I guess I expected some business lesson or a conservation speech.

As best as I can recall, here is what he said: *"More than anything else, fly fishing helps me realize that failure is an event, not who I am. I have failed, a lot, in life, and fly fishing. But failure doesn't define me. It just reminds me that there's still more to learn, more to be done about conservation, more fish to catch."* And with that, he finished his loop knot and made a perfect Spey cast to the far side of the pool.

Wisdom is not a product of schooling but of the lifelong attempt to acquire it. ~Albert Einstein

I got involved in the fly fishing industry through an early retirement scheme put in place due to a pending merger. The scheme helped fund a new business for those of us about to retire, and for me, since I always loved fly fishing, I started a fly fishing travel company, taking people to the best salmon fishing areas. And it was through fly fishing with many different customers that I got the opportunity to manage lodges and fishing beats on the Ponoi Peninsula in northern Russia, lodges in Canada, and finally, become CEO of Loop Tackle.

Fly fishing attracts interesting people who are open to new ideas and like solving problems. And they tend to interact with other fly anglers more openly than with other people. Most of my fly fishing industry opportunities have come through encounters with other fly anglers and helping them solve problems. I think fly fishing and solving problems go hand in hand.

~*Gordon Sim*

Building strong and trusting relationships is an essential leadership skill that pays dividends in multiple ways. Most relationships begin with each party having something in common, which sets the foundation for open conversation and sharing experiences and ideas. And it's incredible what can happen when two fly anglers meet and how that unique chemistry can change lives and spark new ideas.

Retired PepsiCo CEO Donald Kendall says he would never have gone to work for PepsiCo had he not been on a salmon fly fishing trip to Nova Scotia after a World War II stint as a Naval aviator. While on the

East Coast, he decided to stop off for a job interview. The man doing the hiring turned out to be an avid fly angler, gave Kendall a job as a fountain-syrup sales representative, which started his eventual rise to CEO and the merger with Frito-Lay, one of the most successful corporate marriages.

Kendall was CEO for 21 years and paved PepsiCo's entry into Chile by developing a fly fishing friendship with Chilean bottler and media magnate Agustin Edwards. A similar fly fishing friendship paved Pepsi's way into movie theaters.

I was an eager young man when I headed to Wise River, Montana for a job at The Complete Fly Fisher lodge as handyman, fly tier, shop clerk, bartender, driver, and yard boy. Anything to be able to fish the glorious rivers of Montana.

One morning while I was on yard duty pulling and raking weeds, the lodge owner was about to depart with guests who had flown in the afternoon before for the famed Salmon Fly Hatch on the Big Hole River. The guests, two couples, were VIPs and the lodge owner was to be one of their guides. But he was visibly irritated. The second guide hadn't shown up yet, and the lodge owner, a former soldier who had spent time in a German prisoner of war camp, had a strict rule about timeliness.

A little while later, the second guide came roaring up in his dirty pickup, towing a drift boat, and jumped out. He wore in a dirty tie-dye T-shirt, shorts, flip-flops, and a 12-inch tall black Top hat. The lodge owner quickly sent him packing and turned to me. "Get your gear. Your guiding today!".

Fortunately, I knew my way around a boat and had fished the river several times before. We had a very productive day fishing, and I was even able to help the wife improve her casting and catch quite a few nice fish as well.

All the time, the man, who turned out to be the CEO of Burlington Northern Railroad, never once mentioned the late start or the fact that it was my first guiding experience. It seemed like he wanted me to be successful, and he not only fished hard but kept encouraging and complimenting me on my fishing and guiding skills.

As I think back on that experience, he could have been angry and upset at having a punk kid as a guide after spending all that money and time on the trip. Still, he showed me that real leadership is about making people and situations better, no matter the challenge. It's a lesson I have used every day since. My wife and I now own and run that same lodge.

~David Decker

I was an avid golfer for many years, but when I first stepped into a pair of waders and then stepped into a Colorado river, I knew right then and there my golfing was over, and my fly fishing addiction had begun. I hung up my clubs and never looked back. ~Tate Cunningham

I am always amazed at the extraordinary people one meets while fly fishing. There is something unique in the DNA of those who chase fish with flies, and I am humbled to have been able to share that week in Iceland with three very special fly fishermen, Jack Hemingway, Orri Vigfusson and John Green. In the presence of real leaders, it's not difficult to learn life lessons.

I was in high school, and my best friend and I were fishing in a small Georgia trout stream with Mips spinners and cheap casting rods. We weren't having much luck when I looked down the river and saw a very elegantly dressed older gentleman with a bamboo fly rod, and he was catching lots!

I screwed up my courage and we went over to talk to him. I had never seen a fly rod before and wondered how he could be so successful. For the next hour, we stood there like statues, speechless and dumbfounded as he told us why he became a fly fisherman, how it made him feel to be so connected to the river and the outdoors. He told us about entomology and how it was important to understand the river's insect life, and he educated us on fish behavior, biology, and ecology.

I walked away from that encounter feeling as if I had met a genuine wizard. The Merlin of fishing. It was like watching someone rub two sticks together and create fire! I told my friend that from now on, I was going to become a fly fisher. Somehow his passion, knowledge, and insight into the fish and the river lit a spark in me, and I have been trying to learn the art and science of fly fishing ever since.

~*Capt. Skip Zink*

I've seen how fly fishing changes the angler, how connecting to wild fish in unspoiled landscapes affects every one of us. Whatever distractions complicate our lives evaporate under the influence of profound waters and untamed fish. I've also observed how angling can impact communities, offering new strategies to protect indigenous homelands. ~Oliver White

In a fascinating book about fly fishing and life, *Life As A River*,[31] Michael Marx tells how fly fishing on the Roaring Fork River in Colorado helped save the destruction of the old growth rainforest in Malaysia from Mitsubishi Corporation's logging operations. And it came from an unlikely friendship between Marx, head of the International Boycott Mitsubishi Campaign at Rainforest Action Network (RAN), and Dick Recchia, Senior Vice President of Operations for the US subsidiary of Mitsubishi Motors.

That day on the Roaring Fork taught me that even in battle, always look for a way to connect with your opponent as a person. Find something in common. As we fished together that day, we both realized the other was a pretty decent person and could be trusted to do the right thing. The river and sharing a great day of fly fishing allowed us to interact as people, not adversaries.

~Michael Marx

When I was in grad school my dad died, and to deal with my grief and loss, I dropped out of grad school and headed to Ennis, Montana, to fly fish. At that point, all I wanted to do was catch lots of fish and be alone in the outdoors. I lived in a small travel trailer parked in an out of the way area near the river and fished every day. One day I came back from the river, and another trailer was parked next to mine. It towed a drift boat. I figured I have another trout bum like me as a neighbor.

The next morning, I met an elderly couple in their 70's outside their trailer. He was a retired Episcopalian Bishop from the southwest, and he and his wife decided to become fishing bums for a while. I figured I would teach this old man how to fish, but I didn't expect to be taught so much about life from this unlikely fishing couple.

We fished several years together, and more often than not, the wife rowed the drift boat while we fished. And he was what I call a Stage 4 fly fisher. That is, he was way past just catching lots of fish. To him and his wife, fly fishing was about the journey and mentoring others in the life lessons from fly fishing. To me, he became a role model for my personal and professional development. At 70 years old, he still had a child-like excitement and enthusiasm for fly fishing, and most days he kept fishing long after I was exhausted.

Over the years, I absorbed life lessons just being around him and observing his actions and attitude more than his advice. He had a significant influence on me, and a few years later, he officiated over my wedding.

~Joe Dilschneider

Saltwater fly fishing is very different from river fishing or lake fishing. First, the almost constant wind, the sun and heat, and the fish are usually bigger and stronger, requiring different techniques, flies, and rods. Yet every encounter contains a learning opportunity.

When a problem comes, be nice to it, because it tries to teach you something. Look at problems as teachers: Get to know them very well. Make the problem an opportunity rather than a negative thing. ~Klaus Obermeyer

I was Tarpon fishing with Rick Pope, the founder of Temple Fork Outfitters and designer of TFO fly rods, when our guide pointed out what he said was a school of Tarpon up ahead. I was on the bow and ready to cast when I realized they were giant Jacks, not Tarpon, and I was not prepared for that size of fish, or their strength.

When I hooked into a huge Jack, Rick took control of the befuddled guide, and after realizing the guide was not going to move the boat to chase after the school of Jacks I had hooked into, he turned his attention to me. All through the fight, he gave me an advanced education in the physics of fly rod design and how to use the rod's best aspects to land big fish. I learned the best angle to keep the rod, allowing it to work efficiently, and which angle provides the most strength.

We landed that fish and had excellent dinners for four straight days. I came away from that experience not only with a better understanding of the physics and dynamics of fly rods but a greater appreciation for the science behind some of the fabulous equipment we now have in fly fishing. And now, as a multiple business owner, I am keen to dig deeper into the rules and principles of business and leadership. The more I understand why and how, the better I can lead, and fish.

~Jen Ripple

Leadership is not always about the heroic act of making a significant strategic decision or winning a takeover battle. Leadership shows up every day, in many ways. And the lessons learned from fly fishing can be directly applied to multiple leadership situations. And no situation is more challenging than the COVID-19 global pandemic facing all of us.

I learned a valuable leadership lesson one day while I was watching an elderly gentleman on the South Platte River. I watched him for what seemed like hours as he targeted one large trout holding in a difficult riffle to fish.

He treated that fish with the utmost respect. He didn't rush his casts. He watched and thought about how best to present the fly. It was a study in respect for the fish and a master class in fly fishing.

Recently I was able to put that lesson of respect and appreciation into practice. To keep our online business going during the COVID-19 pandemic, we needed to bring back a reduced warehouse crew. They each volunteered for the job out of respect for the company and our customers. They didn't rush to get the job done and go home. They took extra care with each order to make sure everything was right.

> Every day I would go out into the warehouse, watch them work for a few minutes, and then tell them how much I, the company, and our customers appreciated their care and expertise. I felt good, they felt good, and I know the customers felt good receiving their product on time.
>
> *~Brad Befus*

If you think back over your life as a fly angler, business executive, parent, or whatever your chosen path in life, it is probably no surprise that the best lessons have come as a result of encounters with others. A teacher, a good friend, a colleague at work, even a stranger that said or did something that had a profound positive impact. There is an old saying that goes: *"When the student is ready, the teacher appears."* And much of leadership development is about being ready to learn.

> When I get a chance to go fly fishing, I like solitude, and I often fish alone. I recall one day I was swinging for steelhead near a bridge. When another angler showed up, I cursed under my breath and wished he would leave. However, he noticed me fishing, walked up on the bridge, and pointed out a huge steelhead resting in the current. He guided my casts to where I was able to hook and land that fish. When I looked up, the guy was gone.
>
> That incident changed my thinking about encountering strangers. I learned that another person could make my fishing trip even better. And I can help out someone else and make their trip better. Both on the river and at work, remember that the next person you meet might lift you up, and you might lift them up too.
>
> *~Bern Johnson*

CHAPTER 12: Encounters That Change You

Photo courtesy of ©Christian Bacasa

Chapter 13

YOUR LEADERSHIP TEAM
– FLY FISHING BUDDIES

The two biggest decisions in life are
who you choose as a spouse,
and who you choose to fish with.

Chapter 13:

YOUR LEADERSHIP TEAM – FLY FISHING BUDDIES

One thing becomes clearer as one gets older and one's fishing experience increases, and that is the paramount importance of one's fishing companions
~John Ashley-Cooper

What I look for in a team member is the ability to wade into complexity. To think through the problem, gather available information, ask lots of questions of others, and develop multiple scenarios as possible solutions. The most dangerous approach is only to have one solution.

And when my friends and I go fly fishing, we constantly share information, try new approaches, give each other feedback on what's working and not. More often than not, this agile approach lands on the right rigging and fly combination much quicker than if we each tried to solve the problem alone.

~Josh Dees

In business, the importance of a leadership team cannot be underestimated. The days of the solitary CEO knowing everything about the business, customers, and the competition are long over, especially in multinational companies with staff and customers across the globe. Plus no single individual can keep up with the rapid rate of technology and its impact on customers and business models.

Leaders of companies that go from good to great start by getting the right people on the bus, the wrong people off the bus, and the right people in the right seats. ~Jim Collins, Good to Great

I pick the senior leaders for my company based on three criteria. And I came up with this formula after a horrible experience where I founded a software company. Because I was unsure of my own capabilities of running a company, I brought in an older, experienced person who made a sizeable investment, gained controlling ownership, and influenced who we hired on the management team. I said horrible experience because we clashed on things like culture and leadership style, and I was ultimately booted out.

As a result, I came up with my own personal hiring formula. I first look hard at myself. What skills or knowledge do I lack that my company needs? I understand sales and customers but don't have much knowledge about manufacturing, the retail industry, or finance. I then start networking and talking to people. I ask a lot of questions and always ask who they would recommend. I'm looking for people with passion and character, as well as skills and knowledge.

Next, I go fly fishing with them. And I always send them a free sample of our new product. Then I wait to see who comes back to ask more questions and who seems passionate about our product, journey, and the opportunity. I want people who "self-select" to be a part of this company, not just hired guns.

~Scott Wilday

The people we look for to join the Trxstle team are not necessarily experts in business or manufacturing. We are looking for people with passion for the outdoors, openness to new ideas and learning, a drive to continually improve our products. And they must be respectful of the sport of fly fishing. And we fish with each one before making a hiring decision. -John Smigaj

The senior leadership team has the most influence of any group on the overall performance of a business. They set the strategy and company goals, make investment decisions, and manage large teams of people who manufacture products and service clients and customers. Yet in my experience, most senior leadership teams are not a team, and lack of team alignment means they can often work against each other to benefit their function or division, especially since resources and budgets are often tight.

While everyone agrees that teamwork for a common objective is critical for business success, in most companies, the organizational structure, budgeting process, and incentive compensation policies can conspire against effective teamwork at the top.

When Alan Mulally became CEO of Ford Motor Company in 2006, he was the first non-automotive person in the company's history. At that point, the company was broken. The Ford stock price had fallen to a low of $5 a share, its debt was at "junk" status, and 2006 would go down as the worst year in its history with a $12.7 billion loss. And then, in 2008 the global financial crisis hit. Ford headed toward bankruptcy.

Mulally and the senior team refused to take government bailout money, like the other US auto manufacturers. Instead, they crafted a recovery plan called "One Ford," which laid out new objectives and a new culture. However, new strategic plans don't change behaviors. The old Ford culture was a collection of strong functional silos and independent regions, plus infighting at the top for scarce resources and budgets.

Mulally had a choice to either change the players or change the old Ford senior executive compensation policy that rewarded function or division performance and not overall company performance. Mulally implemented a straightforward compensation policy for all senior leaders; their total bonus compensation would rest on the global company reaching or exceeding its strategic turnaround objectives! The team pulled together and implemented a stunning turnaround during the eight years Mulally was CEO.

If I can't go fishing with one of my buddies, I'd rather go alone. Who you spend time fishing with is an important decision, and who you have on your senior leadership team is equally important. ~Craig Langer

I like to fish with self-starters. People who are competent and accountable and have a "get on with it" mindset. When we fish, we fish hard, but we also share information and tips along the way. And the same is true for the people we choose for our management team. I don't need to over-manage those with a high level of personal accountability. Everyone has their strengths and special capabilities and just get it done. Yet when we do come together, it's to share information and work on our business's future.

~Tate Cunningham

Talent wins games, but teamwork and intelligence win championships. ~Michael Jordan

There were three of us on a self-guided fly fishing float trip down the Goodnews River in Alaska. My younger brother, whom I often fish with, and an acquaintance of mine from town, whom neither of us fished with before. He was a keen talker with lots of fishing stories, as well

CHAPTER 13: Your Leadership Team – Fly Fishing Buddies   163 as tales of his wild escapades in Hollywood as a back-up musician for rock bands in the 70's. We were all looking forward to a memorable trip catching Silver Salmon, Rainbow Trout, and good camaraderie.

The fishing was great, but the camaraderie started badly and went downhill from there. Instead of helping with camp duties, cooking, or gathering firewood, he quickly set up his tent and started drinking whisky and smoking a joint. The communication and atmosphere got tenser and tenser as the 6-day trip continued. Polite suggestions to help soon turned into shouts. Then came the last straw.

On the final day, we were camped down near the river's tidal basin and had been catching a few salmon to put in the cool box and take home. It was early morning, and I was fishing on the other side of the river with one of the boats, and our "buddy" and my brother were at the river's edge getting rigged up when a large Grizzly appeared at streamside about 300 yards away. The bear walked upriver towards camp - obviously, the smell of fish and food scraps on his mind.

My brother shouted to get the other boat ready while he ran up to camp to collect the cool box full of fish. He got the box, turned around, and our "buddy" was rowing like a bat out of hell across the river, eyes wide as saucers with fright. We both yelled at him to turn the boat around, but he just kept rowing.

Finally, after several more shouts, he came to his senses, rowed back, and my brother got in just as the Grizzly came into camp. It was a good thing that event happened on our last day; otherwise there might have been murder on the Goodnews! Needless to say, we never fished with him again.

~Donald Childress

Surround yourself with positive people who are going to push you towards greatness. It would be best if you choose the people around you wisely because they will have a significant impact on your potential and how successful you become. ~Warren Buffett

Fly fishing is about much more than just catching fish. The old adage that a bad day of fishing beats a good day at work has a lot of truth. And those we choose to fish with can turn a skunked fishing day into a pleasant and memorable experience, or a twenty-fish day into a nightmare. Out on the river with good friends, many life problems get discussed, advice given, and ideas shared.

Our work at ELAW is helping partners around the world protect communities and ecosystems through law and science. Collaborating with partners across borders to take on environmental abuses demands a common ground of trust and respect. We must build trusting friendships and solidarity to work together to prevent environmental abuses, especially when facing governments and multinational corporations with more money and more lawyers.

Building strong personal and professional relationships takes time, but I have discovered a short-cut: I take partners fly fishing. Imagine taking a German or a Honduran grassroots environmental advocate in a wooden drift boat down Oregon's McKenzie River to catch steelhead, one of the strongest fresh-water fish, and also one of the hardest to catch.

When we first get in the drift boat, I usually give my guests a health warning: "Be prepared. Catching a steelhead will change your life!" To them, it seems impossible that on such a large river, using a small hook decorated with feathers, fur, and thread; attached to a nearly invisible line and a fragile rod, that we can not only find and attract such a big fish, but hook and land one as well.

It almost seems like a fantasy. But the look on their face when they actually hook one, are able to land it, and hold that powerful wildness in their hands, is a special moment. After catching a steelhead together, we have a powerful shared experience that is the foundation for a strong personal and professional relationship. And at the same time, they get to experience the beauty of a healthy, wild river that is at the core of my commitment to protecting the environment.

~Bern Johnson

That which is most desired in (a team) is oneness and not sameness. Sameness is the worst thing that could happen to (a team). To make all people the same would lower their quality, but oneness would raise it. ~Stephen S. Wise

Over the years, I have been a part of and built several leadership teams. I will always remember what Horst Schulze, CEO of Ritz Carlton Hotels, told me when I worked for him. "You can teach people all kinds of skills, but you can't teach them to be nice"!

I really took that to heart, and for me, a great leadership team must have exceptional skills, but also be nice people. To create results in the highly competitive business world, a leadership team needs to enjoy each other's company, trust each other, and feel comfortable to speak openly and honestly.

And the same is true about who I fly fish with. Nothing can ruin a beautiful day on the river than the wrong fishing partner.

~Todd Aaronson

*While I enjoy the solitude of fishing and figuring things
out by myself, surrounding yourself with kind-hearted and
passionate anglers is essential to growth as an angler. And,
make sure to fish with people who are better than you because
you'll **always** learn something new. ~Matteo Moretti [32]*

*To me, leadership is about serving the team. It's better to be the
rudder at the back of the boat than the tip of the spear. ~Josh Dees*

My company, Velocity Global, is now six years old and growing like crazy. I chose my senior leadership team when we were a start-up. This was a significant risk since we were developing a new business model and a new category of international business. I needed a team that had the right functional skills and expertise and would be able to grow with the company.

And that's where my experience of fly fishing came in handy. First on my list for a fly fishing buddy is character and second is a thirst for learning and growing. And those are the same traits I looked for in my start-up leadership team. Of course, they must have the technical and functional skills, but so do hundreds of people. However, not everyone has the strength of character it takes to help build an international business where video conference calls often happen at 3am in the morning. And since the company is on a fast growth track, they needed to be open to change, open to learning new skills and capabilities, and open to personal growth.

~Ben Wright

*The road trips to and from the river are the most valuable
part for me. It's the time to really talk about what we learned
and develop strong bonds of trust and friendship that are
difficult under everyday situations. ~Brian Wetter*

Fly fishing has taught me so much about myself, people and leadership. As the owner of a destination fishing lodge in Belize, the lodge is only as good as our staff. My role is to hire for character, provide the best tools and equipment, provide continuous training and personal development, and allow them to do their jobs without micromanaging. It's my job to find out what motivates each individual and help them succeed.

And in fly fishing, it's the same. I have to assemble all the elements required for a proper presentation and the right fly for the area we are fishing. And I have to motivate each fish I am targeting to chase and eat that fly, which means I have to think about that individual fish and not try and treat every fish the same. A large bonefish at the head of the school behaves very differently from the middle or the edge. And as I release that fish back into the water, I know I am helping to preserve and further develop the entire fishery.

~Ali Gentry Flota

Photo courtesy of Sekarb, iStock

Chapter 14
STEWARDSHIP AND SUSTAINABILITY

There is no business to be done on a dead planet.
~David Bower

Chapter 14:
STEWARDSHIP AND SUSTAINABILITY

Hard to say what's better... the tug or the release.
~Casey Males

Do well by doing good.
~Benjamin Franklin

When I was in college, my girlfriend and I would drive to Sheep Creek, camp for several days, float the river, and fish for beautiful Brook Trout. One time under a log jam, she hooked into a huge fish. It was a joy to watch her land it, smile, and then release it back into the river.

We loved floating the river, cooking dinner on an open fire, looking up at the beautiful night sky and seeing thousands of stars, talking and laughing and singing along with my guitar, sleeping in the camper (and more), waking up and booking breakfast, and doing it all again. The whole pristine river environment was magical.

When I went back 10 years later, the forest surrounding the river had been logged right to the banks of the river. Erosion silted up the river. The banks no longer had steep undercuts to hide the fish. There may have been fish in the river, but no hiding places, pools, riverbanks, log jams, or riparian areas to support insect reproduction. I cried.

That event played a significant role in inspiring me to transition from my career as a corporate and trial consultant, making lots of money, to volunteering to advise the Rainforest Action Network. I became one of their Board members and successfully led the first international environmental boycott of a major company for destroying rainforests.

~*Michael Marx*

Over many years of guiding, I noticed that those rivers with some form of regulatory management held more fish and were healthier. That's what got me into a career of trying to influence watershed policy and management. -Paul Hoobyar

When the Apollo 17 astronauts took that iconic picture of planet earth on December 7, 1972 from a distance of 18,000 miles, it changed the way we look at our planet and our role as stewards of "spaceship earth." Over millions of years, our world evolved as a complex, interconnected ecosystem with all the elements in a dynamic balance. However, it is obvious we humans have upset that balance, sometimes to the point of doing irreparable damage to the environment and our future health and wellbeing.

The litany of environmental abuses and ecological disasters at the hands of businesses and governments is long and painful. As a result of environmental abuse, we now face our most serious environmental challenge - global warming and climate change. More than 77% of CEOs and CFOs of the world's largest companies recently acknowledged that their firms are not prepared for the adverse impact climate change will have on business and humanity. Whereas weather-related disasters and flooding were previously seen as natural acts and had little effect on share price, more and more shareholder groups view such property damage and social disruptions due to poor environmental stewardship and bad leadership.[33]

*Our research at Emerger Strategies shows clearly that as a business
moves aggressively towards executing sustainability strategies such
as, carbon neutrality and zero waste, and actively uses social media
to make customers aware of their commitment, there is a significant
increase in customer loyalty and repeat business. ~Rick Crawford*

There are a growing number of leaders, both in business and
government levels, and concerned and proactive global citizens
who realize it is time to balance progress with sustainability
and stewardship.

To me, the future of both business and fly fishing is bright. Why?
Because there is a new generation coming into the executive ranks
and into fly fishing who have a much greater appreciation for the
outdoors, for conservation, sustainability, and diversity and inclusion.

The baby boomer generation focused on growth at any cost,
and the environment and society suffered in many ways. Today's
leaders, entrepreneurs, and fly fishers are much more attuned to
the world as a fragile ecosystem where business, communities,
and the environment must coexist. And with more women entering
business and fly fishing, they are also getting their children involved
and learning to appreciate the importance of that balance between
business, society, and the environment.

~Jen Ripple

*I am very excited about the transition from the Baby Boomer
generation to the Millennial generation. Their concern
for the environment and sustainable business practices
just might help right the planet. ~Dan Michels*

The concept of stewardship is critical to both the sport of fly fishing
and global business. **Stewardship** is defined as taking responsibility

CHAPTER 14: Stewardship and Sustainability

for sustainable development shared by all those whose actions affect environmental performance, economic activity, and social progress, reflected as both a value and a practice by individuals and organizations, communities, and competent authorities.[34]

My journey towards helping businesses achieve carbon neutrality and zero waste began when I was hired as a waiter at a guest ranch in Wyoming just out of college. My roommate was a fly fishing guide and keen conservationist. I loved fly fishing and was headed for a life as a trout bum until I read two books that opened my eyes to the importance of sustainability and stewardship. The first was **Let My People Go Surfing**, by Yvon Chouinard, the founder of Patagonia, and **Getting Green Done** by Auden Schendler, Vice President of Sustainability at Aspen Skiing Company in Colorado.

Those books propelled me to earn an MBA degree in Sustainable Business and eventually establish my company, Emerger Strategies. We help guides, shops, lodges, and brands in the fly fishing industry attract & retain talent, grow customer loyalty, and improve financial performance, all while solving climate change. I believe it is important for the fly fishing industry to lead sustainable business practices and move towards carbon neutrality and zero waste. No fish means no customers.

~Rick Crawford

Our goal here at El Pescador is for our guests to leave a better angler and conservationist than when they arrived. And with a grin that lasts for weeks after. ~Ali Gentry Flota

Indifly is a nonprofit organization that Al Perkinson and I formed in 2014. Our mission is to help create sustainable livelihoods for indigenous communities by teaching them how to use fly fishing as a form of income. The result is low-impact tourism that drives dollars and creates meaningful and permanent conservation efforts.

Far and away, this is my favorite thing to work on. It all started with a small village named Rewa, deep in the interior of Guyana. Now we are working on similar projects in French Polynesia and Wyoming.

~Oliver White

In fly fishing, stewardship refers to how we care for the natural environment such that fish stocks and their natural habitats remain healthy and productive. Stewardship in business implies integrating all stakeholders and environmental factors to create a win-win-win solution (win for the company, win for customers, win for communities, win for the environment).

> *The excesses of greed, ignorance, and disregard for the environment damages trust in companies, business leaders, government policies, and even our own aspirations in life. I know there is a way for business to be profitable without damaging our natural environment. ~Michael Marx*

Stewardship is hard work and not always popular, especially with Wall Street analysts who focus mostly on maximizing shareholder value. Yet a few enlightened executives are leading the way. In the words of Paul Polman, former CEO of Unilever, "profit is not a purpose; it's an end product."

During his ten years as CEO, Unilever invested heavily in finding ways to make healthy products sustainably. And they continue to be big supporters of the international charity, WaterAid, bringing freshwater and sanitation to underdeveloped communities. It's not a handout or papered-over CSR. It's responsible business and good stewardship. The healthier and more prosperous a community, the less infant mortality and the more educated people will be. With the likelihood that more people around the world will use Unilever products.

There is no ownership of the future.
There is only stewardship.

Fly fishing taught me about ecosystems and that we live in an interconnected world. Businesses can either coexist as part of that ecosystem or upset the balance and cause irreparable damage. ~Rick Crawford

Another companion at the same lodge in 2000 where I met Jack Hemingway was Orri Vigfusson. Orri was an Icelandic businessman, conservationist, and the inspiration behind the innovative and highly successful North Atlantic Salmon Fund, founded in 1996 to support his salmon conservation work.

Orri is credited with saving the wild North Atlantic salmon from extinction through his strategy of brokering commercial conservation agreements while also compensating net fishermen for not fishing and transitioning them to more sustainable fisheries.

The abundance of North Atlantic netting, habitat destruction, and river pollution over the decades between the 50s and 90s took its toll on the stock of wild Atlantic Salmon. Also, the increase in the number of seals and the spread of infectious disease and escaped fish from salmon farms were additional factors in the depleted fish numbers. Orri's efforts to mobilize various countries' government agencies to lead an international effort saved the wild Atlantic salmon from certain extinction.

Orri was only at the lodge for a couple of days, and the only time we socialized was at the dinner table. It was only five years into his efforts to save the wild Atlantic Salmon, but he was encouraged by governments and donors worldwide. *"The salmon sportfishing community is truly global"* I remember him saying, *"and we are drawing on that community for lobbying and financial support."*

Orri Vigfusson passed away in July 2017, yet left behind a real leadership legacy, brokering massive international fishing rights buyouts with governments and corporations in the North Atlantic, effectively stopping destructive commercial salmon fishing in the region. In 2004, Time Magazine named him a "European Hero". In 2007 he was awarded the Goldman Environmental Prize for his efforts on saving endangered species.

Leadership is not a title or a position,
but a responsibility.

On August 20 2019, 14 Nordic CEOs joined together in Reykjavik, Iceland, to make a public statement about their shared vision and commitment to advance an economy where people and planet can thrive together.

Over the past century, global economic progress has successfully transitioned over a billion people out of poverty and brought several improvements in quality of life. Yet, development has been achieved at the expense of nature and the environment, and many people have been left behind, vulnerable to sudden shocks to our economic system. The impact of the COVID-19 crisis will only emphasize prevailing inequalities, and The World Bank estimates that the pandemic could push another 71 million people into extreme poverty in 2020. Future development must deliver human wellbeing, economic prosperity, and environmental sustainability.[35]

If we fail to embrace sustainability,
we risk sustained failure.

Long-term success requires sustainable results, not just results achieved with a trail of bodies in their wake. Fish caught and released will continue to enrich their environment and provide more sport for others. Managers who respect their human resources produce sustainable results, and recognize that well-treated, engaged employees will in the long run also be the most productive.

~*Victor Lipman* [10]

Leadership, like fly fishing, relies on taking care of our most valuable resources. For a business leader, that resource is the hearts and minds of staff and employees, and the customer experience. For fly fishing, that valuable resource is a healthy stock of wild fish and a sustainable habitat in which to thrive and reproduce.

As business leaders and fly fishers, we must give back, use sustainable practices, and be an excellent example for our company and fly fishing clients. At our lodges in the Bahamas, we spend a considerable amount of time educating not only our staff, but their families, the surrounding communities, and especially the younger generation on the importance of sustainable living and sustainable fishing practices. Our goal is to help them conserve their environment for themselves and future generations.

~*Oliver White*

Catch and release is a common practice within the fly fishing community and now mandated on many rivers as a technique for fish stock conservation. After capture, the fish is unhooked and returned to the water. In the United States, catch and release was first introduced as a management tool in Michigan in 1952 to reduce the cost of stocking hatchery trout. The practice soon took hold as an unofficial standard with fly fishers in areas of growing fishing pressure and risk of overfishing and species collapse. Many prime waters are now designated as catch and release only, and most mandate the use of barbless hooks as well.

The best hatchery is a healthy river.

Numerous studies have shown that catch and release practices create sustainable, growing fish populations and healthy ecosystems. Fish contribute to nutrient recycling when they live out their entire lifecycle, from spawning to death, in an aquatic system. Catch and release practices improve fish populations as well as the whole ecosystem.

At our lodge, we spend a lot of time training our guides on how to educate clients on the importance of conservation and sustainability. Our job is more than just getting the clients to hook and land lots of fish. We see our primary role as teachers and environmentalists. That means explaining why it is important to handle fish properly, introducing them to the importance of preserving the fish and the entire ecosystem. We teach them how bears are a vital part of a healthy salmon fishery and how we are all guests in the wilderness.

~*Dan Michels*

I love to guide beginners because the more people we have out on the water, the more stewards we have to care and protect our rivers and our fish. ~Maddie Brenneman, Colorado Guide

I'm not a dedicated fly angler and really never used a fly rod before I met Bern Johnson, Executive Director of ELAW. Bern invited me to visit their offices in Eugene, Oregon to talk about being on their Board of Directors, as he knew of my passion for the environment and my Board experience. But instead of meeting around a boardroom table, we had our meeting in a drift boat on the McKenzie River fishing for Steelhead.

During that trip down the McKenzie, I realized that Bern wanted his board members to experience how important preserving natural ecosystems was to ELAW. I must admit that hooking and landing an elusive steelhead, then returning it to the river, connected me more deeply to their environmental stewardship cause than any slick PowerPoint presentation or fancy charts and graphs.

~Roger de Freitas

We have reached the time in the life of the planet, and humanity's demands upon it, when every fisherman will have to be a riverkeeper, a steward of marine shallows, a watchman on the high seas. ~Thomas McGuane [36]

Why do I love fly fishing? To me, it's the ability to spend time in a pristine environment where the water and the air are clean and pure. I want my children to have the opportunity to experience that same level of purity. But we must take care of the rivers and the environment for today and future generations. That takes leadership, from all of us.

Also, I want to work in a "clean" business, where there are no accounting or finance games. Where the branding messages accurately reflect the product or service. Employees feel the negative impact of a toxic culture, and it affects their families and customers as well. Creating a healthy culture is definitely the responsibility of leadership.

And that means taking care of not only the people, but the equipment and buildings as well. At one hospital where I worked, in order to save costs, management cut back on regular equipment maintenance and upgrades. You can't cut corners in business or fly fishing and expect to be successful. "Would you want your loved one on that ventilator? Would you want your child to take a drink from that river?"

~Fred Owusu

Will growth in the number of lodges and flyfishing damage the rivers? It's a question each lodge owner must struggle with. What's wrong with small and fulfilled? ~Wade Fellin

Photo courtesy of Yellowstone Valley Women Magazine

Chapter 15

50/50 AND THE POWER OF INCLUSION

*Women have been an integral part of fly fishing since **A Treatise of Fishing with an Angle** by Dame Juliana Berners was published in the late 15th century. Throughout the centuries, women have played vital roles in making the sport what it is today. From rod builders to fly tiers and everything in between. Today's female anglers continue to pave the way.*

~DUN Magazine

Chapter 15:

50/50 AND THE POWER OF INCLUSION

Diversity isn't the same as inclusion. One is a description of what is, while the other describes a style of interaction essential to effective teams and organizations."
~Bill Crawford

A part of effective leadership is developing a platform whereby people can come together as a like-minded community, learn from each other, support each other, and improve themselves. This is what I learned as a successful serial entrepreneur, and it's what I recognized was required for women in fly fishing.

We established DUN in 2013 as a platform for women in all aspects of fly fishing. DUN is more than a magazine; it's a community, a network of amazing anglers in beautiful places, supporting each other and enjoying the sport we love. And the establishment of such a platform has resulted in more women taking up the sport for themselves. It spawned many women-owned businesses in the fly fishing industry, bringing new ideas and new products to market to serve the needs of all types of anglers.

I guess I see leadership as providing opportunities, just as I see fly fishing as providing personal development.

~Jen Ripple

Diverse ideas and inclusive opportunities are essential ingredients in the success of any business. And for a good reason. Numerous studies by the global consulting firm McKinsey & Co. show that executive teams with a high percentage of gender diversity outperform less gender-diverse leadership teams. Having gender diversity on executive teams is positively correlated with higher profitability across geographies and industries due to the importance of strategic and operational decisions made at the leadership level. And executive teams of outperforming companies have more women in line roles versus staff roles.[37]

I believe in the importance of diversity, but not filling a quota by adding more women to Boards or promoting more people of color and ethnic backgrounds. To me the power of diversity is in the creation of a culture of inclusion and equality, where the best candidates and most capable are given the same opportunities, no matter what their color, gender, race, background, or personal situation.

During times of crisis and upheaval, such as the COVID-19 global pandemic, diverse teams are more likely to radically innovate and anticipate shifts in consumer needs and consumption patterns, thus helping their companies to gain a competitive edge.[38]

Ultimately the goal of every leader should be to allow everybody to contribute to the best of their possible potential. To the extent that you're not inclusive, that becomes impossible to do. In an inclusive organization, everyone can contribute and grow, which opens doors to innovation and progress. I've learned that diversity is simply about having a mix of people, but inclusion is about making sure that all of those people feel like they belong.

~Jeff Dailey [39]

Recently, more and more women have assumed leadership of large companies (GM, IBM, Lockheed Martin, Textron Systems) and global institutions (the IMF, the World Bank, the European Central Bank). Thirty-seven companies on the Fortune 500 list currently have female CEOs.[40] Women have also been elected to high office around the world. As of May 2020, 19 countries were being led by a woman.

In this era of rapid technological change, an uncertain global economy, and a growing global health crisis, women bring the kind of leadership skills required to develop consensus and align differing agendas. Those skills include the ability to build strong relationships, a bias for communicating directly instead of following the chain of command, a preference for leading from within rather than from the top, and the ability to engage with diverse perspectives to find dependable sustainable solutions.

Many business associations, such as the National Association of Corporate Directors and the Pan-Asian Leadership group Ascend, are at the forefront of preparing women for roles as Board Directors with education and lobbying efforts.

Likewise, Orvis has been spearheading an industry-wide, women-in-fly-fishing initiative, titled "50/50 On The Water". Special fly fishing courses for women, taught by women, and new equipment and fishing apparel designed especially for women and videos and blogs featuring female anglers, have all helped bring more women of all ages into the sport. As a result, women have become the fastest-growing demographic in the sport of fly fishing. The goal is to have 50/50 parity in fly fishing, and at last count in 2019, they were reaching 37%.

50/50 On the Water is unique to the fly fishing world, and groundbreaking as well. But what's really interesting is how it all started. Not with analyzing fly fishing data or a strategic planning event, but with one of the Orvis VPs, Steve Hemkens, on a fly fishing trip with a female guide, Hilary Hutcheson.

According to Steve, he grew up in a large family, and the boys would go fishing and do outdoor stuff while the girls did "girl stuff". Steve fished with women before, but fishing with Hilary had a significant impact on him. She's a talented guide who's passionate about conservation and sharing the sport with more anglers. When he left that trip he had an 'ah ha' moment. More women in fly fishing would really improve the sport and our conservation efforts. And it makes fly fishing more enjoyable as well.

When Steve came back from his trip, he asked Jackie and me to lead the initiative since we'd already been advocating for more women in fly fishing through our teaching at Orvis fly fishing schools. I like to think of it as he simply unleashed us and gave us the support needed. We spent time interviewing women in the sport about barriers that might exist and what they loved about fly fishing. We then invited a group of female fly anglers to workshops at our annual Orvis Guide Rendezvous to brainstorm how to best launch such an initiative.

It is called "50/50 On the Water," and we are trying to achieve gender parity in fly fishing. The latest statistics show that 37% of fly anglers are women. But it's not just about parity, it's also to make fly fishing more accessible to women and to promote women-specific fly fishing gear development, deliver education & adventure experiences, sponsor women-centric storytelling, create non-profit partnerships, and importantly, build more advocates for sustainability and stewardship of fisheries and the environment. The response has been tremendous from women anglers as well as gear and clothing manufacturers. We are excited to watch this grow. A great example of how far this initiative has spread is at a recent World Domino Championship in Belize, a contestant wore a "50/50 On the Water" logo hat!

~Christine Atkins

*I think fly fishing is an equal male and female sport. There's
no difference in physical ability in fly fishing. Across the board
and generally, throughout my guiding and teaching, I have
found women are better students. They tend to listen better.
They don't try to muscle things. They're more about the finesse.
I think they're perfectly suited to fly fishing. ~Rachel Finn [41]*

Women are not just in back-of-the-house roles, such as fly shops, fly tying and rod building. They are on the front line as guides, lodge owners, casting instructors, and equipment designers.

Right after 911 and the upset and travel chaos that ensued, we realized the traditional all-male destination fly fishing trip would decline and be replaced with more family trips. So, we built family-style cottages at our lodge to encourage more families to fish together. We also give free casting lessons every day to our guests. As a result, we have seen steady growth in families, and women's groups, fly fishing.

Fly fishing is not about strength and muscle power since today's rods and lines are designed for simple technique, not muscle power. And we in the industry need to continue to make the sport more accessible to every one, since the more people who fall in love with fly fishing, more people will push for sound conservation policies and sustainability practices at home.

~Ali Gentry Flota

One of the earliest and most influential female fly anglers was Joan Wulff, regarded as the architect of modern fly-casting mechanics, teaching and videos, and an ardent supporter of women in the sport. With her husband Lee, they founded Royal Wulff Products, offering innovative products including fly lines, backing, fluorocarbon leaders and tippet material, fly line dressing, instructional materials, casting aids, and limited-quantity custom-made bamboo fly rods. In many ways Joan Wulff set the role model for future generations of female anglers.

As a fly-casting instructor, I find teaching men and women to be a totally different experience. Men need to muscle the cast much more, and when most men first meet a female instructor, they usually are skeptical and demand that I show them what I can do with a fly rod. Women don't demand proof that I can cast, they accept that I'm the instructor, and we get right into the basics very quickly. And women tend to understand early on that the rod does the work, not their biceps.

~*Heather Hodson*

We can and should have as many women as men at all levels in the industry, not just in angling, but also in brand management, manufacturing, creative, design and development, conservation leadership, policy, guiding — all these things that make this industry go 'round. Women make our lives better. ~Hilary Hutcheson [42]

Women have long been in the shadow of men on outdoor sports and adventure, yet just as capable. The Orvis sponsored "50:50 On the Water", and my own company, *Mountainist*, along with many other organizations, are dedicated to education, adventure experiences, and storytelling to inspire and celebrate women in the outdoor sports we all love. To me, it's more about inclusivity and opportunity than it is a 50:50 quota.

~*Tana Hoffman*

CHAPTER 15: 50/50 and the Power of Inclusion   187

Fish don't care about the sex, color or race of the fly fisher. All they know is a good cast and good drift from a poor one. Success in fly fishing is color blind and gender neutral. It's competency, capability and persistence that pays off in fly fishing, and the same is true in business and leadership.

Chapter 16

INNOVATION – ON AND OFF THE WATER

*Skills move us forward,
innovation leaps us forward!*

Chapter 16:

INNOVATION – ON AND OFF THE WATER

In fly fishing, innovation is about solving problems for the angler. In business, innovation is about solving problems for the customer.
~Brad Befus

Leadership and innovation have always been linked together. The leader who can't or won't push for innovation is not a leader, but a caretaker. And without constant innovation, the shelf life of a business is short and getting shorter all the time as global competition gathers pace.

More than 70 percent of the senior executives in a survey we recently conducted say that innovation will be at least one of the top three drivers of growth for their companies in the next three to five years. Other executives see innovation as the most important way for companies to accelerate the pace of change in today's global business environment. Leading strategic thinkers are moving beyond a focus on traditional product and service categories to pioneer innovations in business processes, distribution, value chains, business models, and even management functions.[43]

Successful innovation takes leadership since innovation requires change and diverts attention and resources from previously established goals. The leader must have the foresight, and the courage, to reshape budgets, establish new objectives, divert resources, and create performance incentives if innovative ideas and products are to bear fruit. And to me, the most important leadership ingredient is courage. There are no guarantees with innovation, and resources are limited, so funding and supporting a new product or service idea is risky.

Technology can be an incredible enabler, but it is not a substitute for leadership skills, or casting skills. Fly rod technology has advanced tremendously. It's not the rod, it's the holder. Technology will not replace human insights and decision making. -Larry Marsiello

When I engage with highly effective leaders and fly fishers, I find they both have a very similar mindset. It goes like this, and you can almost hear the words inside their head: *"There's always a solution, I just haven't found it yet!"* It's this mindset that keeps them trying new things, tinkering to make improvements, or coming up with a whole new product or approach. They are not content with yesterday's solutions. They are thinking way ahead to what could be. This mindset, along with the courage of their convictions, has pushed innovation in both business and fly fishing.

"Let's go invent tomorrow rather than worrying about what happened yesterday." -Steve Jobs

An excellent way to define innovation is the passion for taking the ordinary, the generally accepted, and making a giant step-change in its effectiveness. What was once adequate, with innovation, becomes spectacularly more effective and useful. At times a game-changer.

Like in the business world, fly fishing has experienced a revolution due to innovation and technology. Technological advances, such as light-weight breathable Gore-Tex waders, new fly rod materials, advanced fly line designs, and fly fishing instruction videos, make the sport more enjoyable for the average sports person. If you want to get technical and specific, you can. Still, it is so much easier for the average fly angler to enjoy the sport thanks to these and many other technological advances and innovations.

And the same is true in business. Technology, especially computer technology and the Internet, makes owning your own business and making a living as an entrepreneur available to almost anyone with an internet connection and an idea to give customers what they want and need. A small village in Kenya runs a successful fly tying cooperative that sells flies all over the world. Individual guides can have access to clients anywhere in the world. Business leaders can speak with their entire global workforce all at once via the advances of video conferencing.

~Pat Pendergast

Believe it or not, digital photography and the iPhone's invention have been of great importance to fly fishing. The ease of taking a trophy shot with the iPhone or digital camera makes it easy to record a photo of your fish, then quickly return the fish to the water. Before digital photography, it took a long time getting a 35mm SLR camera from out of my backpack, take off the lens cap, adjust the settings, focus, and get a decent picture. All the while, fish are stressed. And you didn't know the quality of the photo till days or weeks later when the film was developed and printed.

The first important step in innovation is having the confidence that it is possible. ~Justin Fortier

In the business world, technological advances reduce costs, improve performance, and help solve social and environmental problems. Take the electric vehicle, for example. For decades, the electric vehicle's promise was unrealized, since speed and battery life could never equal petrol vehicles. Cost was a barrier as well. Yet as the need for a replacement for CO_2 emitting petrol cars became more important, passionate people turned their energies to innovative solutions.

And thus, Tesla was born. As I write this, Tesla has a $224 billion market value, greater than Volkswagen, Daimler, Ford and GM combined. A 300+ mile battery range and acceleration near that of a Cobra, along with an impressive human-auto digital interface, makes it a popular option for non-petrol transportation.

Technology, especially computer technology and the Internet, have made owning your own business and making a living as an entrepreneur available to almost anyone with an internet connection and an idea for giving customers what they want and need.

I started working at a fly shop around the age of 13. I was the odd-job kid, and the most hated work was sorting, grading, and bagging feathers, sent by farmers and feather merchants from all over the world, as fly tying material. In those days, fly tying was mainly for those purists who took fly fishing seriously. Since the material was difficult to obtain and somewhat expensive, few people tied flies regularly. The volume of fly tying material sold in the shop thirty years ago was very low.

But over the past few decades, there has been tremendous innovation in fly tying materials. Much of the material used today is synthetic, from chenille for body wrap, sparkle and flash for attractors, synthetic dubbing material, rubber legs and shell-back for scuds and shrimp patterns, and a host of other materials. Also, technology and innovation has made considerable improvements in hook design and sharpness. Another great innovation, and an ecologically sound one, is replacing lead with tungsten for fly tying beads and cone heads.

We sell more fly-tying material at our fly shop by volume and number of items than any other fly fishing equipment. And more and more anglers are enjoying catching fish on flies they tied themselves.

> We sell more fly-tying material at our fly shop by volume and number of items than any other fly fishing equipment. And more and more anglers are enjoying catching fish on flies they tied themselves.
>
> *~Chris Daughters*

A great example of innovation in fly fishing is the Mop Fly. Yep, just like it says, an artificial fly made with materials from a mop.[44] Jim Estes, an experienced and highly creative fly angler from western North Carolina, found a fluorescent green mop at his local Dollar Store. The microfibers of the twisted mop "fingers" were a good representation of the sourwood worms that fell from the trees between June through August along North Carolina trout streams. The microfibers of the mop material moved seductively, in even the slowest of water. It is a deadly fly that has consistently caught fish in rivers, lakes, and saltwater flats around the world in a variety of colors.

If you promote innovation, you may fail.
If you don't promote innovation, you will definitely fail.

Innovation takes insight, and you can't always get in-depth insight from customer surveys. It's important to observe how people behave, shop, and live to find real innovation insights. That's why fly fishing is a great learning ground for innovative thinking and development of new ideas, because fly anglers watch how fish behave and how anglers behave.

Those business leaders who drive innovation use insights from real people, not just surveys. Samsung uses ethnography to test their assumptions about how consumers use their products and then use those insights for product innovation.[45] Even the smallest of innovations can sometimes have a huge impact on customers, and sales growth.

Several foreign auto manufacturers captured the early SUV and Suburban car market in the US by living with families and studying how they used their vehicles. And one of the innovations that delighted customers, and helped drive sales, was the design and placement of cup holders. "Soccer moms" haul several kids home after practice or a game and invariably stop at a fast-food drive-through for snacks and a drink. Big drinks often spill, and the Samsung researchers were the first to determine the importance of cup holder size, number and positions.

Nissan have scanned different sized containers into their computer system so that when they design a car for North America, they can ensure there is space for two 32-ounce [950-millitre] drinks, space in the door for a half-liter water bottle, and in the back seat there's additional space for more drinks and water bottles.[46]

To me, innovation, either in business or fly fishing, does not come about in one giant leap. It merely starts with the firmly held belief that there is a new opportunity. You may not know exactly what that new innovation is, but you know in your gut that there's a big opportunity for improvement, or even a breakthrough to a new level. For example, in my company we are working on a model to show how sustainability and profitability can both coexist in modern agriculture.

Once I have a solid belief, I start small. I call it finding one thread of understanding that will lead to a bigger level of insight and understanding, and so on. With this technique we progressively learn more and more, which we use to move our innovation insights to the next level.

And it's the same technique I learned in fly fishing. When I am trying to get to a hard to reach spot on the river where I am confident some big fish are holding, I look for the first step that will get me to the first spot closer to my goal. Then I survey my surroundings and find the second spot while learning more and more about the terrain, the risks, and the possible approaches. And by the time I get to that final spot, I have mentally figured out exactly what I need to do to catch those fish.

~Justin Fortier

Innovation often comes from outsiders who can see new ways of doing things. Insiders often get institutional blindness. At Loop Tackle many of our key people are outsiders, and as a result, we have rebuilt the brand on multiple rod and reel innovations. ~Gordon Sim

Innovation comes from a variety of different sources. Pushing and trying hard is usually the least effective means of ideation. It's the passion for solving problems combined with a curious, open mindset that acts like a magnet for new ideas and innovations. Like-minded friends and a couple of drinks also help!

The innovation for our new product, Rock Treads, came from two separate events which combined in a moment of insight, helped with a glass or two of Maker's Mark bourbon whisky. As keen fly anglers, we were fishing in a river with a very slick, slate bottom, and my fishing partner kept falling in. His wading boots, even with steel studs, kept sliding on the rocks. It was a frustrating day for both of us, and the incident stayed in the back of our minds as a problem to solve one day.

Later we were fishing with an aluminum canoe, which we had to drag over a series of rocks. We both noticed that the aluminum canoe didn't slide easily over the rocks. It kept gripping the surface. Again, another hard day of fly fishing and a glass or two of Maker's Mark in the evening. At that point, it dawned on us that aluminum is softer than most metals used for wading boot studs, and Patagonia had just come out with a wading boot designed to include aluminum bars on the bottoms. But you had to buy the whole boot.

So the concept for Rock Treads, aluminum discs you could mount on any wading boot and arrange in any pattern, was born. I think serious fly anglers, like those serious about building a business, are curious people who enjoy figuring out solutions to thorny problems. It's the innovators that move society forward.

~Forrest Rogers

"You can't solve a problem on the same level that it was created. You have to rise above it to the next level." ~Albert Einstein

CHAPTER 16: Innovation – On and Off the Water

Chapter 17

PLANNING, AGILITY AND THE UNEXPECTED

To every person there comes in their lifetime that special moment when they are figuratively tapped on the shoulder and offered the chance to do a very special thing, unique to them and fitted to their talents. What a tragedy if that moment finds them unprepared or unqualified for the work which could be their finest hour.
~Winston Churchill

Chapter 17:

PLANNING, AGILITY AND THE UNEXPECTED

For a soldier trained at West Point as an engineer, the idea that a problem has different solutions on different days was fundamentally disturbing.
~General Stanley McChrystal

As I write this, the world is in an unprecedented global pandemic caused by the rapid spread of the novel COVID-19 virus. Every organization, institution, nation, community and individual has had to react to this situation without the luxury of preplanning or forethought. While business agility was a consulting buzzword months ago, it is now a reality and a necessity for our businesses and institutions' survival.

A lot of people fish like they are following a SATNav. Just following a set pattern or approach they always use. Success in fly fishing and leadership is to make your own path. If you always follow the same pattern, you don't learn as much. And learning is fundamental to leadership. ~Gordon Sim

Being agile in business means quickly adapting your organization and people to a new way of working. In this case, social distancing, home working, furloughs, and for some, business closure. It's not planned, it's a reaction for survival.

In baseball and in fly fishing, I've learned that I'm not always in control, but I've always got options. Total control is a myth in baseball, and certainly in fly fishing, probably in most professions. ~Rick Porcello

Agility works best when your choices are based on fundamental principles and not spur of the moment reactions. And this is where leadership comes into play. As the leader, your reactions will impact hundreds, if not hundreds of thousands, of individuals, inside your organization and beyond into the community and country.

Success today requires the agility and drive to constantly rethink, reinvigorate, react, and reinvent. ~Bill Gates

In times of uncertainty, it is the job of leadership to show courage, make tough decisions, be prepared to alter course as new information becomes available, and reassure people that together they will find or create a solution works for everyone.

Those leaders who embrace crises with speed and agility have several things in common:

- They listen first, gather information second, create multiple scenarios, and then respond
- They are quick to protect the health and wellbeing of their employees and customers
- They are not afraid to restructure budgets, objectives and reallocate resources
- They nurture close relationships with customers, vendors, and suppliers
- They think beyond their own business and engage with their communities
- When new information becomes available, they have the courage to change quickly.

Although I can't anticipate all potential contingencies, the more I plan and think through different scenarios, when the unexpected does happen, I am better able to respond quickly and with more confidence. ~Paul Hoobyar

In business and fly fishing, nothing ever goes smoothly. The perfect strategic plan suddenly isn't so perfect when new competitors or a new technology appears. And that monster trout didn't get the memo that he's supposed to stay hooked, stay out of the swift current, away from the log jam, and come to the net quickly.

Every fish has one last run in them. Don't take the first success as a final win. In fly fishing or business. ~Michael Marx

I find that success in fly fishing and business both require a good amount of serious preplanning. There's nothing worse than being on the water and not having the right equipment. And equally, there's nothing worse than being in a meeting and not being prepared and not having the right expertise in the room. ~Richard Commodore

I got a phone call from an elderly man who wanted to hire me to guide him on a fly fishing trip for a day on our local river. We agreed to meet on the river at 7:30 am. He was a fairly good fly angler but didn't seem to be in a good mood, even though he was catching good sized fish.

So, I decided to engage him in some light conversation to elevate the mood in the boat. Just as I started, he asked me, "What kind of Hot Sauce to you prefer?" I was taken by surprise but answered with my favorite Texas style brand. He short back, "Wrong answer! Did you not Google me? If you had researched me before this trip you would know that my family owns the biggest and best hot sauce company in the world!"

We fished in relative silence for the rest of the trip. I was embarrassed and got zero tip as well. But I learned a priceless lesson about dealing with people and especially about business and leadership. Never go to a meeting unprepared; always do research beforehand on the topic and people in the meeting!

~Tucker Horne

Be prepared for what you know and work hard to be prepared for what you don't know. ~Richard Commodore

Early in my fly fishing career, I fished in a couple of remote locations where I brought a minimal amount of gear and wound up unprepared for issues such as a major storm, cold weather, high water conditions, or a sudden hatch. I soon learned that I needed to go about the same thorough pre-trip preparation for fishing adventures as I did for my surgical procedures if I wanted a successful trip. Thus, I started making checklists (like before surgeries) of rods, reels, lines, leaders, flies, clothing, sunscreen, etc. And I would review my list several times before a trip to be well prepared for most eventualities. In fly fishing, as in orthopedic surgery, it pays to be well prepared.

In cases where I was the lead orthopedic surgeon, I was in charge of the entire procedure, with others' help and support in the operating room. I guess you could say I was the team leader and, in many ways, responsible for everything, including adequate preparation ahead of time.

With this in mind, I would preplan for unforeseen eventualities. I spent a reasonable amount of time well before the operation to review in my mind the potential problems that might arise and what equipment I would need to solve these during the procedure, then put them on my pre-op checklist. Thus, if difficulties might arise, we would have the appropriate equipment available to handle the problem.

~Gary Forster

Fly fishing teaches people to be organized and methodical in their approach. And that is an excellent leadership principle as well. I use checklists to run our two businesses, and also when I am getting ready for a fishing trip. ~Forrest Rogers

CHAPTER 17: Planning, Agility and the Unexpected   203

To the business leader and the fly angler, agility is more than just a quick reaction and changing plans. It's about having materials, equipment, and capabilities available if and when they are needed. Many business leaders see inventory as a cost and drain on cash flow. Over the past several decades, inventory stocks have been reduced in favor of just-in-time supply chains. An efficient approach, assuming stability of the economy and material sourcing. Which has proven to be a wrong assumption.

The global economy has been anything but stable or predictable. Yet P&L driven executives have clung on to the practice of minimal inventories, as have many governments, thus reducing stockpiles of equipment, spares, and supplies needed in emergencies.

Logistics is a follow on to preparation. "Tactics are for amateurs, logistics are for pros," is a saying I believe in. What it means to me is thinking through the day and not "winging it." From the time you get up until you end your day, it's all a logistics exercise. Getting one thing from one place to another and having that one thing there when you want it. It sounds a lot like planning, but it is more than that. It is identifying the components, acquiring them, and having them available.

~Tom Sadler

The secret of all victory lies in the organization
of the non-obvious. ~Marcus Aurelius

I was fishing on the Pitt River in British Columbia for Sea-Run Bull Trout. So far, I had little luck with the fish, although they were obviously in the river. We moved downriver to a large pool, and my guide told me to tie on a Sculpin pattern. "That's what we always fish in this pool."

I thought, it's a big pool probably holding big fish and big fish like a big meal. So, I pulled out a Mouse pattern I had bought from my local fly shop. The guide was adamant that a Mouse fly wouldn't work and said rather loudly that Bull Trout don't eat mice. And in all his years of guiding, they never fished a Mouse fly on this river. Just not the right pattern.

But it just seemed like the right thing at the time. I persisted, tied on a large Mouse fly, and on the second cast the water erupted. I was hooked into a monster Bull Trout.

Fly fishing has taught me the importance of agility and lateral thinking in my business career and to search for solutions to problems from other industries. So now we are making Jet Fuel and Omega-3 from algae to eliminate the harmful environmental impact of fossil fuels and antibiotics use. Success in fly fishing and leadership are both about agility and lateral thinking to solve problems.

~*Graham Ellis*

*For the man sound in body and serene of mind, there is no such thing
as bad weather; every sky has its beauty, and storms which whip
the blood do but make it pulse more vigorously. ~George Gissing*

I have found in both successful leaders and fly anglers a unique ability to pivot their approach when things aren't working or when there is an external change in business conditions or water conditions. Rather than push harder and double down on their original strategy, they quickly rethink their approach in light of new and compelling information.

The COVID-19 global pandemic is an excellent example of how some leaders quickly pivot their organizations to take advantage of the new opportunities. Then there are those business leaders that choose to cut costs, retrench, reduce spending, and try and ride out the storm. It is estimated that the majority of businesses and organizations are in the latter camp, choosing to try to survive rather than pivoting to thrive.

We own Crazy Creek, which makes a very popular range of portable chairs for camping, backpacking, and outdoor events. With the onslaught of COVID-19, our sales almost dried up due to the lockdown, cancelled outdoor events, and national parks closing. But as keen fly anglers, we are used to responding with speed and agility by switching flies and lines and approaches when one type of fishing isn't delivering.

So, we realized that kids in schools could have classes outdoors or in the gym, which is safer than being crammed together in a classroom. We quickly pivoted our marketing strategy to help schools and teachers solve the problem of keeping children safe using comfortable, durable portable chairs. Success in difficult and changing times is all about mental agility, just like in fly fishing. There is always a solution; it just takes learning to think differently.

~Forrest Rogers

Those who fail to plan, plan to fail.

Photo courtesy of Santy.

Chapter 18

CONTINUOUS LEARNING AND PERSISTENCE

Fly fishing is you versus you. Every time you go to a new river, you learn something new. You get better every time you go, but it will always be a challenge. It's forever evolving, so you can push yourself constantly. When you put yourself out there and don't give up, it all comes together.
~Michaela Merrill

Chapter 18:

CONTINUOUS LEARNING AND PERSISTENCE

Fly fishing and leadership are both long games.
There is no shortcut to success in either.
~Margot Page

Leaders are never done learning and always seek to improve themselves.
They are curious about new possibilities and act to explore them.
~Jeff Bezos

Leaders and fly anglers are interesting creatures. They come in all shapes, sizes, colors, and backgrounds, and to categorize or lump them into a single description is futile and pointless. There is, however, one characteristic that is ingrained in most of those we consider leaders, and fly anglers. They are persistent, lifelong learners.

Fly fishing teaches you that failure is just part of learning and improving. And our first product at Trxstle was a huge failure as the internal lining we chose kept damaging the rods and ripping. And it was worse since it was our only product. My partner and I wondered if it was going to be game over.

But the huge amount of feedback and support we received from our customers gave us the impetus to fix the liner issue, and several other minor problems as well. Someone once said fail stands for ***First Attempt In Learning.***

~John Smigaj

If I catch more salmon for the week than my fishing partners, it's because I start earlier, move quickly and find new water, use attractor patterns, and generally have my fly in the water more than most people. More time on the water creates more experience to draw from with every new day of fishing. ~Gordon Sim

Real leaders are curious and always eager to learn more. They work overtime to understand more about their business, their employees, and about themselves. They read voraciously. They Google things they are curious about, like the origins of certain words, sports statistics, the backgrounds of famous people in history. It's not a search for perfection, but about being better at whatever they deem to be important. And they are persistent at it.

Persistence is a key principle in fly fishing and leadership. Persistence creates consistency in casting and eliminates false casts that disturb the water and fish. Consistency is leadership is all about doing what you said you were going to do and showing up on time, every time. With consistency in fly fishing, you begin to trust yourself and your skills, and with consistency in business, people know they can trust and rely on you. ~Greg Keenan

One of the leadership principles I have internalized through fly fishing is persistence. And I learned it at an early age. One Christmas, when I was 11 years old, I received a starter fly fishing kit from Santa (AKA, my Dad). It was all wrapped up under the tree, but I knew what it was since I had been pestering my dad for months after watching him use a fly rod.

Even though it was December in Wisconsin, bitter cold with deep snow on the ground, I assembled the rod and ran outside to practice casting. I was terrible. The line kept wrapping around my arms, neck, legs, and if I did get a cast off, it fell in a jumbled heap about 3 feet away. After being so excited and visualizing myself as a great fly fisherman, I came inside embarrassed and frustrated.

But every day I practiced. And I would ask my dad for tips. I slowly improved until my casts were straighter and longer, and I started to feel a sense of accomplishment and confidence.

Some people get jobs where there is a standard career path. Not so for me. All my life, I have worked with groups of people and leadership teams on teamwork, goal setting, and leadership. And my manual for that has been my interpretation of that early lesson from fly casting: "persistence." Observe, try, reflect, modify, try again, reflect, modify, try again, and continue. The great thing about fly fishing and leadership is that you get plenty of real-time feedback and ample opportunities to learn, relearn, and improve.

~Michael J. McNally

Real leaders don't always make the right decision, but they always learn.
Dedicated fly anglers don't always catch fish, but they always learn.

I learned myself through fly fishing. ~April Vokey

Leaders and fly anglers are both adventurers at heart. Not content with the same river or the same product for too long, they constantly look for new, interesting, and challenging pursuits. To the fly fisher, it's the section of a river they heard about that takes days of hiking to reach. To the business leader it's the new way to make their product more sustainable, cost-effective, and easier to use.

> In fly fishing, we may fish the same line and the same fly, but it is critical to mend the line to take advantage of different currents and locations. It's a way of maximizing your chances of success. And the same is true in business. We need to continually adjust our marketing approach and services in order to match different nationalities and customer requirements.
>
> *~Ben Wright*

Good casts come from experience,
and experience comes from bad casts.

I started fly fishing about eight years ago on a trip with friends to the Fraser River. Someone loaned me their old fly rod, and I tried to figure it out. I didn't know any fly fishing knots, just tied on a fly my friend gave me using a regular overhand knot. I had never cast a fly rod before, but I got the line out into the river after many clumsy attempts. Believe it or not, I caught a fish.

Words cannot describe the joy I felt. I have been semi-professionally dancing all my life, and catching that fish was the same kind of delight I feel when dancing. It was very emotional, and at that moment, I was hooked. I wanted to become a real fly angler.

I'm a very driven person, but also very stubborn. I need to figure out things for myself because I learn faster and deeper that way. Instead of taking casting or fly fishing lessons, I started going fishing with people way better than me. While I felt like a clutz around them, they were really helpful with tips and suggestions.

Developing as a leader is about putting yourself in challenging situations, taking on the difficult tasks no one else wants, using your existing knowledge to get started, getting feedback, adjusting, and continuing to move forward. Fly fishing taught me about the importance of feedback and making adjustments quickly.

~Michaela Merrill

Recently I stayed at the Dearborn Inn near Ford headquarters in Michigan, just outside of Detroit. The inn was built by Henry Ford, as was the airport to land Ford executives and clients from all over the world for meetings and conferences. I didn't know this before I visited the Ford Museum close by, but Henry Ford and Thomas Edison were contemporaries, and early in his life, Henry Ford worked for Edison.

Both Henry Ford and Thomas Edison were life-long learners, curious tinkerers in all sorts of areas. Ford was curious to learn more about transportation and motor vehicles and production techniques, modern town planning, social issues, and all sorts of human endeavors. Thomas Edison was the ultimate curious learner, attested by the fact that he had 1,093 US Patents to his name. Besides the light bulb, Edison also invented the motion picture projector, the phonograph, and the alkaline storage battery.

> *I am not overly impressed by the great names and reputations of those who might be trying to beat me to an invention. It's their 'ideas' that appeal to me. I am quite correctly described as more of a sponge than an inventor. ~Thomas Edison*

Often on a leadership team, there are individuals who stand out for their curiosity and openness to learning. Unfortunately, many senior executives become infected with the "know it all" disease, which of course is ultimately fatal, since the world is changing so rapidly. As leadership coach, Marshall Goldsmith is fond saying, *"What got you here, won't get you there."* More often than not, a year or two later the open sponges for knowledge and ideas are promoted. Wherever they reside in the organization, the curious learners always wind up making a positive difference.

The moment you stop learning, you stop leading. -Rick Warren

In my view, the best leaders are also the best learners. I enjoyed a military career, both enlisted and commissioned, and would observe some individuals voraciously taking advanced courses in subjects such as leadership, history, sociology, and psychology. These individuals continued to get promoted, often reaching the highest enlisted and officer ranks. Then I would observe some others sitting back, enjoying their rank and privileges, and progressing no further. I quickly figured out why our highest ranked folks got to the top.

~Dusty Sprague

Those who volunteer for tough assignments get noticed. The volunteer is not always successful, but the fact they are willing to take up the challenge is not overlooked by senior management. Who would you rather promote, the person who plays it safe or the one who engages a challenge head on?

If you are the smartest person in the room,
then you are in the wrong room.
If you are catching lots of fish easily,
you are on the wrong river.

90% of the time, if you volunteer, you're gonna be stuck doing some sh*tty job. But now and then, when you volunteer for something, it's gonna be something pretty awesome. -Junior Navy Officer

Over several years I got to be pretty good fishing on my local trout waters. I knew the hatches, the holding water, and the best times to fish. My casting was perfectly tuned for the conditions. However, I went to the Bahamans on a bonefish trip and was a total clutz. I didn't catch a thing, and my casting looked like a child throwing spaghetti.

That experience had a great impact on me as a business leader. You can be highly effective in one company, and move to another company, even in the same industry, and find yourself struggling. The key to effective leadership is the ability to slow down, reflect on the current situation and be open to learn an additional set of skills.

~*Fred Owusu*

In 1881 The Galveston Daily News described the vested business interests in Galveston as behaving like "big fish in a small pond." The phrase stuck in American literature ever since. There is a lot to be said for being the big fish in a small pond, especially in business. It's much less risky; other people don't challenge you as much; you can talk more, do less work, and still get away with it. What's not to like?

The only way to build bigger muscles is to lift heavier weights! ~Arnold Schwarzenegger

If you want to grow your leadership skills, then the comfort zone is the last place you want to be. You need to try new things, volunteer for difficult assignments, read twice as much as the next person. Leaders are never 100% certain about the road ahead. There is always the risk of failure. Certainty or security is not an option for leaders, but determination and preparation are!

My Comfort Zone – A Poem
Author Unknown

I used to have a comfort zone where I knew I wouldn't fail.
The same four walls and busywork were really more like jail.
I longed so much to do the things I'd never done before,
But stayed inside my comfort zone and paced the same old floor.

I said it didn't matter that I wasn't doing much.
I said I didn't care for things like commission checks and such.
I claimed to be so busy with the things inside the zone,
But deep inside I longed for something special of my own.

I couldn't let my life go by just watching others win.
I held my breath; I stepped outside and let the change begin.
I took a step and with new strength I'd never felt before,
I kissed my comfort zone goodbye and closed and locked the door.

If you're in a comfort zone, afraid to venture out,
Remember that all winners were at one time filled with doubt.
A step or two and words of praise can make your dreams come true.
Reach for your future with a smile; success is there for you!

Stretch outside of your comfort zone and watch yourself grow. Get out of the small pond into a big pond if you want to learn and develop your capabilities. It's the most challenging assignments where you learn the most; about yourself, other people, human dynamics, creativity, and of course, leadership skills. The reason few people volunteer for tough assignments is its hard work, and they don't understand the value that can come from tough assignments.

In September 1983 I visited the River Piława in Northern Poland. It was one of the best grayling rivers in Poland, especially for large fish. I did not catch any fish on the first day, but some of my friends, whom I met by the water, had a brace of nice fish. Seeking an understanding of why they caught fish, and I didn't, I opened the fish stomachs trying to understand what they were eating. Although the bellies were full of food, I did not know entomology. I was frustrated. How can I catch fish with artificial flies if I cannot recognize their food? After my return home, I immediately started studying books on entomology.

At that time, there were very few entomology books in Polish for a beginner. Soon I became a frequent guest in the library of the Institute of Zoology of the Polish Academy of Sciences in Warsaw, "devouring" all the literature on aquatic invertebrates. Within two years, I had a reasonably good knowledge of them. In 1986 I bought a professional stereoscopic microscope, something that was seemingly impossible in a communist country at that time.

From then on when I met other anglers by the water, the situation was reversed – they wondered why their creels were empty, while mine was full. I became a scientist studying the natural food of various fish species, not only grayling and trout but also whitefish, perch, pike chub, ide, and dace. The art of imitation in fly fishing had a specific meaning for me – perhaps less from the point of view of an exact imitation, but rather understanding the feeding behavior of the fish, something that very few anglers are aware of or bother to care about.

~Stanislaw Cios

Some days, the fishing is epic, and other days you can't buy a strike, let alone a fish. Both are learning opportunities for my clients and me. ~Capt. Skip Zink.

Many anglers get excited at the hookup and first run of the fish, their imagination exploding with the thought of a beautiful, big brown trout on the other end. However, they are crestfallen when they see that it's just a White Fish. But think about it this way. You used great skill casting, moving the fly, and setting the hook. You should recognize and embrace that talent you have developed, irrespective of what kind of fish you caught.

We all have huge plans for catching a monster Brown Trout or landing that big business client or deal. Yet life doesn't always deliver on your Plan A. But don't discount Plan B or C. They are steppingstones in the river of life, and every success, large or small, adds additional skills and confidence. You did everything right to catch that White Fish. So, keep doing everything right, and you will eventually land a "whale"!

~Joe Dilschneider

Fly fishing is a sport that combines serenity, triumph, and frustration in exactly the right proportions to teach lasting lessons about life and everything in between. ~Tom Teague

Real leadership is a long game. Quick wins are for managers. The value of leadership lies in being able to look over the horizon, to work on issues three to five to 10 years into the future, while others keep the day to day activities moving forward. Some call this aspect of leadership "chasing a vision". Others refer to it as pulling the organization forward into the future.

I remember when Amazon first started as an online book seller. With my default day-to-day focus, I was extremely skeptical. After all, I loved browsing around book shops and usually bought a book only after leafing through a few pages to see if it piqued my interest. And I was also leery about giving my credit card information to anyone over the internet. I doubt if I was the only one thinking like this back in 1995. But Jeff Bezos was looking over the horizon and pulling us all into the future.

A friend and I decided we needed a fly fishing trip together and arrived at the boat ramp at 5am ready for a great day on the lake. We both fished hard all day without a single fish. Actually, without even a strike. And we constantly tried different flies, different leader lengths and fishing depths. Nothing.

Then at 6 pm, after putting in over 12 hours of solid fishing, something changed, and the fish began showing and feeding on the surface. We fished for another three hours till it was dark, and it was honestly the best fly fishing of my life.

I have often thought about that experience since it taught me the importance of playing the long game and putting in the time. It's only through effort and persistence, and trying new things, that real learning, and maybe even some form of mastery happens.

And in my role as a business leader for a large health care company I gravitate towards working on big, strategic business challenges that won't be solved in one or two quarters. My boss calls them 20-year, career-long problems. And with every little win along the way, my capabilities and confidence at solving big, long-game problems grows. A friend calls this "relentless incrementalism".

~Brian Wetter

My advice for those who want to become better leaders is the same as for those who want to be better rugby players or fly anglers: Learn the principles, practice, play the game, then keep improving yourself and the game. ~Clement Booth

In fly fishing and leadership, those that rise to the very top of their chosen profession have a thirst for learning everything there is to know about their subject. In fly fishing, it's not just casting or matching the hatch. Its understanding the Ulta-Violet color spectrum and how water clarity and weather affect the fly's visibility to fish. It's learning fish biology. It's ecology and ecosystem dynamics.

And the same is true for those who rise to the top in business. They don't just know their products, costs and profit margins. They want to learn everything about their current and future customers. They study psychology and neuropsychology to understand better how to deal with people. Successful leaders read constantly, and not just business books, but biographies about great leaders and books about emerging technologies. All these bits of information link together in the subconscious and surface when it's time to solve fishing challenges and business problems.

~Mac Brown

There is nothing noble in being superior to your fellow men. True nobility lies in being superior to your former self. ~Ernest Hemingway

CHAPTER 18: Continuous Learning and Persistence

Chapter 19:

WELL-BEING AND HEALING

I discovered that while fly fishing, I was in another place.
In this place there was no cancer, no pain and no fear.
~ Reel Recovery Participant

Chapter 19:

WELL-BEING AND HEALING

Fly fishing helped me heal!
~Christian Bacasa,

Facing divorce, being a single mother and fighting breast cancer,
I fell into a deep depression – until I discovered fly fishing.
~Sue Hunter [47]

I was facilitating a Reel Recovery fly fishing weekend retreat in Pennsylvania. One of the attendees was a man in his 50's, suffering from brain cancer. He drove a long way to attend, and it was obvious he was angry and depressed. His prognosis for recovery was not good, and he told us his anger and depression came from the real possibility that he would not be able to attend his eldest daughter's wedding, his second daughter's college events, or his youngest daughter graduating from high school.

He said he had been living in the dark since his diagnosis and couldn't find a way out. Everything seemed dark and hopeless to him. He even confided in me the first evening that he was contemplating suicide.

But we got him out on the river with a fly rod in his hand, and quickly he caught several fish. He was beaming from ear to ear the entire day and even started joking with the other attendees. That evening, he shared with the group that he felt the light for the first time since his diagnosis. "You guys have saved my life. From now on, I am going to live in the light, no matter what happens!"

~Stan Golub

Even before the COVID-19 global pandemic upended company business plans and people's lives everywhere, lack of exercise, poor eating habits, obesity, and the rising stresses of modern living contributed to a growing number of unhealthy employees. And the prolonged lockdown, working from home, and continued layoffs has created a crisis of depression and poor health.

And as every business leader knows, poor health and mental well-being among workers contribute to low productivity and higher medical insurance costs. Research shows that the cost of poor productivity is 2.3 times higher than medical and pharmacy costs.[48] And a recent CIPD survey found that declining mental health and stress were the top two causes of long-term absence in UK workplaces.[49]

Fly fishing brings joy to people in so many ways. Just the back and forth motion of casting is joyful, as is catching, netting, and returning a beautiful trout to the water. There's also camaraderie, friendship, and the added joy of being with others in the outdoors. Fly fishing is also a mindful activity that causes us to forget about the past and the future. It brings us to the present. Healing can only occur in the present and that's where joy lives as well. That's how fly fishing can heal us and help us find a path to post-traumatic growth.

~Todd Degrosseilliers

Employee health and well-being are no longer a nice to have. They've become a leadership responsibility. Health and well-being programs run the gamut from gym memberships, in-company healthy canteens, day-care centers, group exercise classes, safety training, stress-management classes, and many others. All focused on helping employees reduce stress and improve mental health and well-being.

When leadership gets serious about worker safety and well-being, everyone wins, and employees begin to take accountability for each other's safety and well-being as well. Focusing on health and safety can positively benefit the entire organization, improve the working culture and the bottom line, as Alcoa discovered.

In 1987, Paul O'Neill, formerly the President of International Paper Corp., became CEO of Alcoa Aluminum Corporation. While he could have focused on cost-cutting and acquisitions to boost performance, O'Neill realized that worker safety and employee well-being personally touched everyone in the company. When employees feel safe and secure at work, they are more engaged, innovative, and productive.

Before O'Neill became CEO, nearly every plant had at least one accident per week. After he and the leadership team built and executed a strategy of safety everywhere, every time, for everyone, some facilities would go years without a single employee losing a workday due to an accident. Alcoa's employee injury rate fell to one-twentieth the US average. When O'Neill retired as Chairman in 2000, Alcoa's market value had increased from $3 billion in 1986 to $27.53 billion in 2000, and net income increased from $200 million to $1.5 billion.[50]

Corporate health and wellness programs are more popular than ever. Yet many are poorly designed, poorly supported by upper management, and don't always reach those with the most significant physical or psychological needs.

I would honestly say that fly fishing and being out in nature has saved me and put my life on a positive path. When I was young and emotionally lost, fly fishing found me and saved me.

When I was a troubled teenager, fly fishing and the stories of my elders found me and saved me. Being a wife and mother is difficult but again, fly fishing has given me the ability to see the grateful side of life and not dwell on the problems or my own failings. If you are open to learning and growing as a person and a leader, fly fishing is willing to teach you.

~*April Vokey*

During this COVID-19 pandemic, fly fishing has helped people refresh and rejuvenate through being out on the river and in nature. It's the best prescription for mental health. ~Jackie Kutzer

Fly fishing has proven to be a great way to improve mental health and physical well-being. Returning servicemen with PTSD and physical health issues, recovering cancer patients, young adults with little hope, and those of us dealing with the stresses and strains of modern life have benefited from a day on the water fly fishing.

One day I was meeting a client for a guided fly fishing trip. "Look," he said before we got in the boat, "I just want to fish and get away from it all." Just by looking I could tell he was more than tense and upset. He seemed sad. Fortunately, I knew enough about guiding by then to keep my mouth shut and not pry, learning from experience that he would say more at some point. We had a good fishing day, not spectacular, but the client was 100% absorbed and enjoying the river, the outdoors, and the fishing.

When we sat on the tailgate of my pickup and were taking off waders at the end of the day, he opened up. "I am so glad I went fishing today. A fly fishing trip was just what I needed. You see, I'm down here with some college friends to bury a good friend. I can't thank you enough for today's fishing, and for just letting me fish. I didn't think about tomorrow or the funeral the entire day. You helped me escape the pain through fishing. This was therapeutic. Just what I needed."

That experience impacted me. You never know what is going on for people, their pain, or their situation, but I now have great faith in the healing properties of fly fishing and a day on the water.

~Tom Sadler

Fly fishing puts people in touch with themselves, to step out of the rat-race they have created and see themselves and their future differently. And for those leading a growing business, stepping back, reflecting, and taking honest stock is critical for their well-being, as well as their business.

I've always been a full-throttle person. Always active, always on the go, and even more so with my business, Mountainist. I was always on the move attending women's outdoor dirt biking, snowmobiling, and skiing events, encouraging women to experience the thrill of mountain sports and providing them with good quality equipment for rent. I was really looking forward to the 2020 season since it would be the first full year as a business after a strong start in 2019.

Then two unforeseen things happened. First the COVID-19 pandemic hit and conferences and outdoor events were cancelled. And secondly, a cancerous melanoma spot appeared on my back, and I had a large section of skin cut away. So, no business and being relegated to the couch for weeks. Sheer agony for a Type A person like me.

After I spent a few weeks healing and worrying at home, I decided to go fly fishing. Fly fishing was always a secondary sport for me, but since I couldn't get out on a dirt bike or trail bike yet, it seemed like a safe and easy way to get outdoors for some fresh air.

As soon as I put on my waders and stepped into the river, my overactive brain started to slow down. I fished for three hours and waded about half a mile downriver. The entire experience was one of calm, focus, and clarity. Right then, I realized that just as I was in unfamiliar territory fly fishing on this river, my business was facing an uncharted and unfamiliar situation. I needed to slow down and rethink my life and my business. Up till that moment, I had been trying to force my old business model to work.

I came back from that fly fishing trip refreshed. I refocused on pivoting my business from gear rental to building an online community where women's stories and examples of courage and risk-taking would inspire others to try new outdoor adventures. We're no longer just a rental company, but a community for women to do more and be more. The time spent fly fishing helped me slow down, focus, and pivot my lifestyle as well as my business.

~Tana Hoffman

Several non-profit organizations use fly fishing retreats to support those suffering from debilitating and life-threatening illnesses such as cancer, and the physical wounds and emotional scars in returning servicemen and women. Staffed with volunteers who pair up with the attendees, the whole outdoor experience and the camaraderie is a way to step out of their troubles. In many cases, it's the beginning of the emotional and physical healing process.

*For women who have had surgery or radiation as part of their
breast cancer treatment, the gentle motion of fly casting can be good
physical therapy for increasing mobility in the arm and upper body.
Couple that with the emotional benefits of connecting with nature,
and you've got powerful medicine. ~Casting for Recovery website*

I volunteer as a fishing buddy to cancer patients who come to the group, Reel Recovery, to forget their pain and affliction and experience the healing power of nature and fly fishing. And being a cancer survivor myself, I know how they feel and how much better they feel after being out on the water with a fly rod in their hand.

One day I was paired up with a gentleman with extensive cancer. We were on a pond, and I was coaching him in fly casting when he hooked and landed a huge Rainbow trout. He was over the moon, but when we released the fish he turned and said, "I don't want to fish anymore. I'm tired and frankly, I'd just rather talk."

We sat at the edge of a beautiful pond in the afternoon, and he talked about his life and his joys, family, and accomplishments. It was clear he just wanted to escape from continually thinking about his condition, doctor's appointments, and medications. Fly fishing is much more than an escape from the real world. It helps people heal, physically and emotionally.

~Dave Engen

Leadership is about more than just growing a business and making profit for shareholders. Real leaders take extra steps to move society forward. There are numerous organizations established that use fly fishing to support and help heal those with life-threatening illness, physical or mental wounds suffered in wartime, and children with emotional or family problems. Three of them, Project Healing Waters Fly Fishing, Reel Recovery, and Casting for Recovery, have numerous national and even international chapters, staffed with caring volunteers, providing free fly fishing retreats.

> *I withdrew into silence about my diagnosis. Casting for Recovery*
> *helped me turn the corner with my diagnosis. I was surrounded by*
> *the warmth, care, and love of the staff and volunteers for a most*
> *extraordinary weekend. ~Casting for Recovery participant*

In every case, these organizations were established through the courage, compassion and drive of individuals in leadership roles who saw a need to help make the world a better place. That's the highest level of leadership.

My mother died of cancer without getting much support or help, and I wanted to spare other women that lonely experience. It was that, plus the full healing and well-being experience of fly fishing, that led me to become a founding member of Casting for Recovery. We started in 1996 to help women with cancer gain physical and emotional relief.

At the time, there was no "sport for health" model. So we assembled a bunch of "make it happen" women and created the business model that is now used by most other organizations. It's a relatively simple model, using retreats, donations, and caring volunteers to provide a free, stress-free weekend experience for those with trauma, physical handicaps, and debilitating illnesses.

~Margot Page

> *Fly fishing and the entire outdoors experience has proven*
> *healing impact of body and soul. ~Faye Nelson*

Sometimes life hits us with things that damage our souls. When this happens, it's okay not to be okay. If we forget this – well - we can lose our way. Sometimes we lack the strength and the willpower to pick ourselves up and return to the fray. That's when we need help to find what we need to get back home.

I was wounded several times in 2004, fighting alongside my men in Iraq during the Second Battle of Fallujah. The result for me was multiple Traumatic Brain Injuries and a long list of orthopedic and balance issues. Fortunately, in April 2015, during a physical therapy appointment, my vision therapist recommended fly fishing as an option for my clinical regimen. That's how I got re-connected to fly fishing – through Project Healing Waters Fly Fishing, Inc.

Fly fishing's wisdom enabled me to see life from a broader perspective. Fly fishing brings joy to people in so many ways. Just the back and forth motion of casting is joyful, as is hooking (on a barbless hook), netting, and returning a beautiful trout to the water. There's also camaraderie, friendship, and the added joy of being with others in the outdoors. Fly fishing is also a mindful activity that causes us to forget about the past and the future. It brings us to the present. Healing can only occur in the present, and that's where joy lives as well. That's how fly fishing can heal us and help us find a path to post-traumatic growth.

~Todd Degrosseilliers

I went to the Retreat, a man ready to give in to my despair and desperation, and now, two months later, my life is full of promise, hope, and the support of new, cherished friends. ~Reel Recovery Participant

 Photo courtesy of Michael Svoboda, iStock

Chapter 20
STORIES AND COMMUNICATION

Stories constitute the single most powerful weapon in a leader's arsenal.
~Dr. Howard Gardner

Chapter 20:

STORIES AND COMMUNICATION

There are two kinds of speakers; those that are
nervous and those that are liars.
~Mark Twain

A leader has to listen with the intent, not just the words, if they are to
truly hear and understand the needs of the individual or team.
An angler listens to the entire environment of the fish to be successful.
~Christian Bacasa.

Effective communication is an essential skill for any leader to master. Whether it be a one-on-one conversation, staff meeting, a town hall meeting, or a global business conference, the ability to communicate ideas and information in a manner that others remember and improve is critical.

Most leaders understand the consequences of poor financial management, but few appreciate the critical importance of communication skills. The Deepwater Horizon oil rig explosion in April 2010 resulted in a massive crisis for British Petroleum and its business partners in offshore drilling. Not only were there 11 deaths, but the oil leak lasted for 85 days, 16 hours, 25 minutes. An estimated 200 million gallons of crude oil flowed into the Gulf of Mexico. A total of 16,000 miles of US coastline was affected, including Texas, Louisiana, Mississippi, Alabama, and Florida, all prime saltwater fisheries. The cost to BP is around $63.4 billion for legal fees and clean-up costs. And then there is the damage to the Gulf Coast fishing industry and tourism.

So, where does communication come in? The then BP CEO, Tony Haywood, gave several disastrous press conferences in which he tried to play down the impact of the explosion, then tried to blame contractors, and then got angry at the press for interrupting his sailing holiday. The Board soon fired him, but the damage was done. The share price of BP fell by over 60%, wiping billions off the balance sheet.

Anyone can communicate, but few connect.
Anyone can cast, but few connect.

In 1995 I worked for a leadership consulting firm. I was a new consultant, and the CEO was also new. At the time, the company was struggling to grow, even though it had great success with its leadership and team building workshops. In just a few years the new CEO built the company into a recognized brand name with a large and successful group of business clients.

I knew he was a fly fisherman, so I invited him on a trip with some of my fly fishing friends and a couple of expert guides one day. It was technical fishing, and we all enjoyed the catching, but what we really enjoyed, and I still remember to this day, was the stories the CEO told around the campfire every night. He was a master storyteller and alternatively had us laughing one minute and soberly reflecting on a life lesson the next.

As a business leader, he was mild mannered and soft spoken, and very respectful of others. But through telling stories at staff meetings, conferences, and training sessions, he communicated information, motivation, skills, and confidence that helped every employee grow and develop, which helped grow the business. Great leaders understand that stories engage the listener and imbed themselves deeply into one's memory banks far more than giving orders or telling people what to do.

~Michael J. McNally

Effective communication is more than just the transmission of information. It's about connecting with another human being that creates a new insight and motivates a positive change.

In 1994 I became a partner with the legendary fly fisherman, author, film maker and master of the Spey cast, Hugh Falkus, in The Hugh Falkus School of Spey Casting in southern England. We had known each other for many years and fished together often. He was in every sense a leader, partially because of his fishing and outdoor expertise, but mostly due to his life experiences, people skills, and teaching techniques.

Celebrities, film and TV stars, along with business executives and mad-keen fishermen and women, stood in silent rapture as Hugh gave his famous Spey casting lessons. People who usually competed for airtime and talked to impress were eerily quiet as Hugh introduced them to the graceful art of Spey casting through humor and stories.

Never once did he lecture or pontificate. Instead, he used the highly effective leadership skill of imparting information through stories that captured the imagination, painted clear mental pictures, and opened the mind with humor. When people are relaxed and laughing, information flows more easily into their subconscious, bypassing those parts of the brain that cause people to tense up.

~Michael Daunt

Leadership, communication, and fly fishing share more similarities than you might think. Here is an example from an evening discussion I had with my good friend, Luciano Alba. Luciano and his father own and run an exceptional fly fishing lodge in the wilds of Patagonia, Argentina. I have fished with him and his father over many years at Estancia Laguna Verde, one of the world's best trout fishing destinations.

Like any lodge owner intent on helping his business grow and prosper, Luciano gives presentations about the lodge and their fishing program at various fly fishing shows and outdoor conferences in the US, UK, and other countries. Like most of us, speaking in front of a crowd is daunting and often scary. So over dinner one evening, we talked about the basics of public speaking, and he asked me for a few tips.

One of the ways I like to share information is through an analogy, which is a comparison between one thing and another, typically for explanation or clarification. For me, the best analogies are those where the listener can personally relate. So, since he was an expert fly angler, I used fly fishing analogies to explain effective public speaking fundamentals. After all, the purpose of a good presentation is to "hook the audience" (pun intended) on your ideas and message.

Here is my list of leadership fundamentals for effective public speaking and communication, using fly fishing as the analogy:

Know your subject: All good fishermen realize that to be successful, you have to master the cast and understand the performance characteristics of different lines, leaders, and tippets.

In terms of public speaking, it is critical to understand your subject matter to draw from a wealth of examples and feel comfortable talking about the subject. To give a public presentation on something you know very little about is a design to fail.

Know your audience: Each fish species is different in their behavior and ecology. Rainbow trout like fast-flowing, highly oxygenated water, while Brown trout tend to prefer slower moving water with lots of weeds for cover. Small bonefish tend to school, while larger ones are more solitary.

Who is your audience? Business executives, middle managers, supervisors, a mixed audience from the South, a young college audience? Each group is interested in different things, and the language you use, the stories you tell, and the examples must match your audience's interests. My tutor, Tom Willhite, used to say that to be a successful speaker, you must start at your audience's level, then move them through stories and examples to a point where you can actively engage them in your ideas and messages.

Talk from an outline, not a script: Those who fly fish understand that having a basic plan when fishing is important since it allows you to bring the right types of flies, the right rods, reels, and clothing. But no fishing expedition ever goes according to the original plan. There are always unexpected events, like weather or broken equipment. Flexibility and creativity are the keys to a successful fishing trip.

The same is true for a public presentation. If you memorize a script, you may deliver all the words in the right order, but it can easily lack emotion and authenticity, and your audience can easily tune out. Let your natural creativity and the reactions of the audience guide your choice of words and stories.

Every boxer has a plan until they get punched
in the mouth. -Mike Tyson

Speak slowly: Fly fishing is not a hurried sport. The best fly presentations use slow, smooth casting strokes that allow the rod and line's physics to do its work. Rushing a cast often results in the line crumbling at your feet instead of shooting out across the stream. And most fishing must be done slowly, especially when swinging a streamer. Moving the fly too fast makes it look artificial rather than like a tasty morsel swimming in the current.

When speaking to an audience, your words can have more inflection and impact when spoken slowly, rather than trying to rush to get through all the material. And it is more impactful to pause often so that the message can sink in, rather than spraying out the words in machine-gun fashion.

Move and make eye contact: When fly fishing, it is important to keep scanning the water and the area for clues about where fish might be or where there is a low branch or log that could snag your fly. The worst fishing technique is to flog the same water over and over again, instead keep moving around, trying different pools and pockets of water.

The speaker who stands still and doesn't make eye contact with the audience members or move across the stage will find his message falling on deaf ears. And making eye contact is critical since you can then read the reaction to your message on the faces of people. Eye contact makes your message more personal. "Wow, it was as if she was speaking just to me!"

Care: Fly anglers care about the fish, the river, and the entire ecosystem. They practice catch and release. They also care about the environment and many anglers come home with trash picked up along the river and the roadside.

> *Nobody cares how much you know until they know*
> *how much you care. ~Thomas D Willhite*

It is pretty apparent during a public speech whether or not the speaker cares about the material, the ideas, and the audience. The caring speaker is enthusiastic, genuine, smiles a lot, and real emotion shows through. The audience feels their caring and responds by listening intently.

It's not just the information that comes from the leader, but the tone, the timing, and the delivery that causes employees to absorb the lessons. Leaders need to bring facts and data to life for the audience to engage and make positive changes.

The exact same principle applies to fly fishing. It's more about the delivery than the actual fly you are using. A perfectly tied fly presented poorly gets a refusal every time. The same is true in sales.

~Oliver White

When fishing in Los Roches for bonefish and tarpon, I quickly learned that movements on the skiff deck scare off the fish or make them so nervous they ignore even the best-presented fly. The deck of the boat amplifies vibrations caused by moving about and talking. Sometimes, in fly fishing and leadership, being silent and staying still is the best way to connect.

And sometimes, the best form of communication is just to let others talk.

Fly anglers tell stories about events that could — except for the lack of believability — be regarded as miracles. One cool night around a fire outside a lodge, listening to funny scotch-fueled fishing stories, I decided to pull out my digital camera and show a photo of a nice trout that I had caught, photographed and returned to the stream earlier in the day.

The other anglers had been telling stories about their arms growing tired from catching so many fish or hooking trout big enough to spit up Jonah. When I showed my (big fish) photo, the stories abruptly ended. The evening turned reflective and quiet. The guy with the single malt turned in early and took his bottle with him. I no longer confuse Story Hour with Show and Tell.

~*Tom Teague*

Chapter 21

CHARACTER

Fly fishing is an excellent way to judge a person's character.
~Forrest Rogers

Chapter 21:

CHARACTER

Leadership is a potent combination of strategy and character.
But if you must be without one, be without the strategy.
~General Norman Schwarzkopf

When it comes to leadership, competencies determine what
a person can do, commitment determines what they want
to do, and character determines what they will do.
~Mary Crossan [51]

To me, the concept of character perfectly sums up great leaders and fly anglers. How do we define character, and why is it so fundamental to good leadership and fly fishing?

Late one afternoon at the end of a hard day of fishing in nearly gale force Patagonia winds with temperatures hovering around 4°C (39°F), my guide and I headed back to the lodge, the heater of the Toyota Hi-Lux pickup blasting. I was longing for a hot shower and a double Scotch, no ice!

My guide for the week was a young (mid-20's) Argentinian who spoke little English but in every way a person of strong moral and social character. He spent the entire day helping me change flies, untangle knots in my line, he cooked lunch in a hut over coals, even fished me out after a dunking in the ice-cold lake. Not a great day of catching either. I was cold, tired, and looking forward to the comforts of the lodge as we drove over the rough gravel road. All I wanted was to get to the lodge, in a hurry.

Suddenly my guide stopped the pickup, opened his door, and ran about 15 yards up the road. I sat and watched. Somehow, he spotted a female Ground-Tyrant (small seed-eating bird) and a brood of six baby chicks in the middle of the road. They are tiny and grey and blended in with the rocky road, making them almost invisible. I didn't even see them at first! He gently shooed the mother and chicks off the road, he went back to look, finding two more chicks hiding among the stones. He carefully escorted them to their waiting mother. He got back in the truck, and we drove on. He said nothing. Just a natural act of character from someone who cares.

Leadership is getting things done with good manners and common sense! ~Commander Stephen Mackay, Royal Navy (Retired)

Excellence in leadership and excellence in fly fishing rely a great deal on the individual's character. And the elements of character that produce excellence in both are surprisingly similar.

One day I was fishing on a river, and an elderly gentleman was fishing about 70 yards above me. He hooked into what looked like a massive fish by how the rod was bent nearly double. I could see he was struggling to land the fish when he called out, "Do you have a net?" I waved yes and he slowly brought the fish downstream.

My net was too small for his monster trout, but when we finally managed to get it into the net, head and tail hanging over the rim, I noticed he was using a tiny, probably size 22 Gnat fly. While I was amazed at this huge trout on such a small hook, I was even more impressed by how he treated that fish to remove the hook and release the fish, all very respectfully and without causing the fish undue stress. We talked for a few minutes after he released the fish, and I was doubly impressed. He was not only extremely humble, but more interested in me and my fishing that day than bragging about his monster trout.

After a short while of talking, he walked back upstream, fished for a few minutes longer, and then was gone. I thought to myself, that's the kind of person I want to be!

~*Michael Marx*

I try hard to live by this fly-fishing principle: What can we learn from the river, not what can the river give us. ~Wade Fellin

One unique aspect of the fly fishing world is that it is an incredibly collaborative and sharing industry. If you are new to the sport, people are eager to help you learn as much as you can take in. And if you are developing a new business in the fly fishing industry, other business leaders are supportive and helpful, sharing their experiences and making introductions to the right people and business partners. Collaboration is the key to growth in the fly fishing industry, and I believe it is becoming more important in the global business world.

~*Jen Ripple*

People who fly fish are, on the whole, highly principle-based, as evidenced by Catch and Release, Barbless flies, and Sustainability practices. And the same is true for real leaders, they are principle-based, not profit based. ~Larry Marsiello

Those with a strong leadership character are trustworthy, and they trust others. Trust is earned by acting consistently, usually based on a set of core principles that put the well-being of employees, customers, the community, and the environment before profits and shareholder returns. As a result of their consistent behavior, employees and shareholders tend to trust and respect their decisions and words.

CHAPTER 21: Character

Without trust and respect, people may follow the leader's decisions, but will not commit their hearts, minds, and full energies.

Real leaders and real fly anglers have strong character traits. And one of those traits is generosity and helping others succeed. I was on my very first saltwater fly fishing trip to the Bahamas for bonefish. I wasn't a very experienced angler at the time, and my gear wasn't the newest or in the best condition. I only had one 8wt rod and one old reel.

On the first day of our five-day trip, I hooked my first ever bonefish. As I was fighting it, my reel fell apart, beyond repair. I thought; Great, four more days in bonefish heaven, and I have no reel.

At the lodge dinner that evening I sat next to a gentleman who was leaving in the morning. He gave me his very expensive Tibor reel and told me to get it back to him when I could. It just so happened we were both from New York City. The reel was incredible, which I did return in good condition. From that time on, we become friends, and eight years later we are still friends and have fished together all over the world.

~Sean Monahan

An excellent fly angler can be trusted to follow the written and unwritten ground rules when they are fishing. They always crimp the barbs in designated barbless areas, and many use barbless hooks most of the time. They can be trusted to speak up when others are circumventing the rules, and their high level of respect for the sport means they pick up after themselves, only wade when necessary, and work to keep fish wet when handling. Their behavior encourages others, and, in many ways, they become a role model of fly fishing leadership.

I've seen competent leaders who stood in front of a platoon and saw it as a platoon. But I've also seen great leaders who stood in front of a platoon and saw it as 44 individuals, each of whom had his hopes, each of whom had his aspirations, each of whom wanted to live, each of whom wanted to do good. So, you must have competence and character to lead them, develop them, and bring them home safely. ~General Norman Schwartzkopf [52]

I am concerned, however, that the fundamental importance of character in business is not only diminishing, but in many cases, discounted. One reason could be that our society and educational system tend to focus on competency, knowledge, and bank account size more than character. And in fly fishing, there is a growing emphasis on the "trophy fish" and bragging rights, sometimes to the exclusion of protecting our fragile rivers and ecosystems.

I used to fish with someone who hated not catching fish. His constant rant when things weren't going well was, "I hate f***ing fly fishing!" He was the kind of person who believed a leader should always be in control, and it angered him when external events negatively impacted his fishing or his business objectives. He constantly pushed himself, and others, harder and harder.

I don't find that attitude a successful way to live one's life. There are many things out of our direct control, but we have to get on with the job anyway. Pushing harder makes my casting fall apart, and pushing on my employees doesn't increase performance or productivity. It's not important what happens, it's how you handle it that matters. And handing unforeseen situations with ease and grace is a critical leadership skill.

~Justin Fortier

CHAPTER 21: Character

Because power corrupts, society's demands for moral
authority and character increase as the importance
of the position increases. ~John Adams

Today, especially in politics and global business, character seems old fashioned and out of place. Yet character fundamentally shapes how we engage with the world around us, how we behave, what we reinforce, who we engage with in conversation, what we value, what we chose to act on, and how we make decisions.

How do you identify a person with character? Listen to them when things go wrong, when the strategy falls short or when sales plans aren't delivered. Did they find fault with their staff, blame external events, or other people, or did they accept their accountability, learn from it, and come up with a different approach?

A critical character trait of effective leaders is accountability. Being accountable means not just accepting responsibility for the problem, but more importantly, stepping up to fix the situation. Verbally accepting accountability without positive action to improve the situation is the action of a weak and ineffective leader.

When quarterly results fall short of Wall Street expectations, a weak leader often puts out a letter blaming the sales and profit down-turn on the economy, unseasonable weather, or a cold snap that keeps shoppers away. Macy's chief financial officer, Karen Hoguet, blamed the company's weakness in the luxury retail market on lipstick. During earnings call on March 26, 2015, Hoguet said, *"We did some consumer research, and the (female) customers said they like going to the off-price retailers because they don't have to put lipstick on."* [53]

And in September 2013, Men's Wearhouse CEO Doug Ewert blamed brides and the number 13 for his company's lousy sales, which fell by 10%. Ewert blamed "numerical anomalies," specifically triskaidekaphobia, or fear of the number 13. According to the company's CEO, women were afraid to get married in 2013 because it could bring bad luck. He blamed the fear of the number 13 for a downturn in tuxedo sales and rentals for grooms. [53]

If you could kick the person in the pants responsible for most of your troubles, you wouldn't sit for a month. -Theodore Roosevelt

And you can tell the character of a fly fisher by listening to them after a "skunk" day. Did they blame the wind, water conditions, or a lousy guide? Or did they talk about the beauty of the fishery and the many things they learned and plan to do differently next time?

Excuses sound best to the person making them up

The future of our planet, businesses, and the sport of fly fishing will be shaped by those with strong character, not big titles.

Several years ago, I was invited to attend a year-end sales conference by a CEO client. Imagine an upscale Florida convention center filled with happy employees who had just blown the doors off their revenue targets. Everyone was in a great mood, and light-hearted laughter could be heard everywhere the attendees went.

On the final evening, it was time for the closing ceremonies, gala dinner and a special guest entertainer. Sparing no expense, the event organizers had reached out to Las Vegas for a well-known stand-up comedian who was guaranteed to have them rolling in the aisles – just right for a year-end celebration.

After a great meal came the awards ceremony with recognition based on the six core values of the company. The Values Awards were given out by the CEO, who took the opportunity to stress the importance of each one of the company values. *"Our values help us produce excellent business results such as we've delivered this year,"* he said, *"and are also the foundation of our everyday behavior."*

Then it was time for the festivities. The lights dimmed, and out walked the guest entertainer to thundering applause. It was apparent he had been briefed on the company and their stellar results since he started with a few light-hearted comments about the products and some of the senior managers. Everything started out great.

But as he launched into his comedy routine, a wave of unease rippled through the crowd. The jokes were funny, but more suited for a 'boy's night out' than a corporate sales meeting. And with each passing joke, the tension grew. People began to look around, wondering if it was okay to laugh – the jokes were crudely funny, but . . .

After two more jokes, the CEO stood up from his table and walked up on stage. He motioned to the stunned entertainer for the microphone. By this time, not a fork was moving. He turned to the shocked comedian and said: *"Thank you. Your services are no longer required. You will receive your fee, but your act is finished. Now, get off my stage!"*

He then turned to the audience. *"I apologize to you all. These jokes do not fit with our values of respect for all people. I am sorry and take full responsibility. I firmly believe our shared corporate values are more important than anything else – they are what make us a great company. I suggest we enjoy each other's company. That's the best entertainment I can think of."* He walked off the stage to a standing ovation.

> *Your real character is not how you see yourself, but how people talk about you when you're not in the room.*

The acceptance of responsibility by those in leadership positions is not only impactful but contagious. In this case, a simple act, taking no longer than two minutes, had a more significant impact on the company culture, employee trust, and respect for management than any speech, any memo, any poster on company values, or any training course. Because of the CEO's character and visible action, everyone realized that values were important. Before he sat down, the word was out on email and twitter to the rest of the company! The culture came to life that evening, and stories of *'THE sales conference'* are still told inside the company, especially to new employees.

What if the CEO had done nothing and let the comedian continue? What if the CEO had fired the Head of Corporate Communications after the event, blaming her?

The price of greatness is responsibility. ~Winston Churchill

Character is developed, usually at an early age. With good role models, mentors, coaches, and guides, those with the desire and propensity for hard work can further develop and strengthen their character.

During the courses and clinics that we run for the kids, age 12-18, on the USA Youth Fly Fishing Competition Team, leadership and character development are perhaps more important than casting and fly selection. We are training great young competition fly anglers and youth leaders, ambassadors for the sport, and future stewards of the environment.

One day at the beginning of a clinic, one of our young members asked me if he could help a new kid who hadn't attended any of the clinics yet. "Can I spend time with him and teach him what I've learned about casting and fly fishing? I think it will help me learn even more by teaching others."

~Tucker Horne

You cannot dream yourself into a character; you must hammer and forge yourself one. ~Henry David Thoreau

I believe the business world can learn a lot from the fly fishing industry. Traditional business focuses on beating the competition through underpricing and other ways to gain an advantage. When I founded a software company in the health care industry, competition was ruthless, and profit was the holy grail.

CHAPTER 21: Character

Now I've got a start-up in the fly fishing industry, and I am amazed at how supportive and helpful people are. They introduce you to others who can help with product development, manufacturing, people with the skills we need, marketing ideas. It's a collaborative industry that cares about people and the environment. Even the big players, like Fishpond and Orvis, have been incredibly supportive of our start-up. Those in the fly fishing industry are passionate about the sport, their products, and making a profit.

~*Scott Wilday*

Watch your thoughts, for they become words. Watch your words, for they become actions. Watch your actions, for they become habits. Watch your habits, for they become character. Watch your character, for it becomes your destiny. ~Lao Tzu

CHAPTER 21: Character

Photo courtesy of ©John R Childress

Chapter 22
IT STARTS AND ENDS WITH HEART

To handle yourself, use your head; to handle others, use your heart.
~Eleanor Roosevelt

Chapter 22:

IT STARTS AND ENDS WITH HEART

*Fly fishing starts way before you step into the river. It begins
with the dream of being there, of making the arrangements,
of talking to friends about an upcoming trip, of gathering
equipment, choosing the right flies, dreaming of that first pull.*

~Ali Gentry Flota

While fishing the North Fork of the Clearwater River in the
Bitterroot Mountains of Montana with my older brother, we
came upon a curious sight. On the bank next to the river was a wooden
cross with an old straw hat stuck on top, and the initials *"DM"* written
on the wood. It was too far from the road to mark a car accident,
and after some discussion, it occurred to us just what this streamside
marker might represent.

Our opinion was, this wooden shrine marked a much-loved section
of the river of an avid fly fisher. We also assumed his fishing friends or
family built and placed the cross and used his favorite hat. It looked
like new construction and would certainly not survive the winter
snows and the high spring water. We both looked at each other, and
the same thoughts passed through our minds. "Not bad for a final
resting place"!

We left the river and were back in Sandpoint, Idaho by 11 pm. I was
definitely exhausted, from the driving, not the fishing. Somehow the
brisk mountain air, the soothing sounds of the river, and the sight
of the little grave marker had healed those parts of my soul that get
bruised through city living.

Several months later I received a message in my email in response to a blog I wrote about the Clearwater trip. It read:

> John. Thanks for your blog and the photo. That is a marker we left on the side of the Clearwater River this year to memorialize my dad, who grew up fishing that river. We lost Dad to diabetes on April 5, 2011, and he is greatly missed. Each year when we visit the North Fork, it brings us closer to him again.
>
> Every year we replace his marker as we know it won't last from year to year. My dad had no happier place on earth. This past year, his mother and brother passed away and we are going back to the Clearwater, spreading their ashes and placing two more crosses.

I often wonder why people fall in love with fly fishing. And it's not the kind of love a football fan has for a team. It seems to be deeper and less about the wins and losses than the personal feeling of connectedness to something bigger. In many ways, fly fishing is an extension of who I am, and also the kind of person I want to become. ~Greg Keenan

A few enlightened business leaders understand the importance of people and heart as the foundation of their current and future business success. Much has been written about Southwest Airlines and its focus on employees and customers. The heart logo on every aircraft's belly and the "Heart sets us apart" tagline has been operationalized into every aspect of their organization. People are at the heart of everything Southwest Airlines does, internally and externally.

And if you think talking about the importance of people, customers and heart is just a PR slogan, look at their business performance. On January 23, 2020, Southwest reported its 47th consecutive year of profitability in a difficult and turbulent industry. Southwest has been the most profitable airline and the only major US airline that hasn't filed for bankruptcy. A remarkable feat in any industry.

More and more business leaders realize that without heart, it is difficult to attract and retain today's young employees, who want to work for a company with purpose. While Southwest Airlines figured that out over forty years ago, it is a key leadership principle that all leaders need to understand and take to heart!

To be successful, you must have your heart in your business, and your business in your heart." ~Thomas Watson Sr.

I was fascinated by the outdoors and fishing as a kid and started fly fishing and tying flies around age 7. I used my dad's old fly rod to cast on the lawn for hours, and my next-door neighbor saw my enthusiasm and showed me how to tie flies. What I remember about those early days was not so much the fishing but building strong relationships with my dad and my neighbor. All my adult life, I have found that fly fishing is more about the great people you meet and the friends you make than the fish you catch.

~Brian Wetter

I think fly fishing finds you as much as you find it! ~Heather Hodson

My great grandfather built a cabin along the Canejos River in southern Colorado, where my family has vacationed for generations. There is a picture in the cabin of me, at 4 ½ years old, with my dad and my first fish. And it was there that I taught my son and daughter to fish. To me, fly fishing is all about family and friends. Catching fish is secondary.

CHAPTER 22: It Starts and Ends with Heart

My grandfather became ill with dementia and didn't remember much of anything. A few months before his death, my father took him down to the cabin for one last fishing trip. He needed help putting on waders and tying on the fly and, to be honest, he was not totally lucid. Yet the strange thing is, once he got the fly rod in his hand and was standing knee-deep in the river, he made perfect casts over and over. I believe the love and joy of fly fishing are inside us and never really goes away.

~*Ben Wright*

People fall in love with fly fishing like no other sport because the experience resonates with every fiber and molecule in us. Fly fishing connects us to the environment, to water – the foundation of life – to people from all walks of life who share a common passion, to guides, to communities, to cultures, and the entire ecosystem. ~Ali Gentry Flota

I'm not very religious, but for years I was searching for something spiritual in my life. Probably like most people who want to connect to their spiritual side but are somewhat repulsed by religious dogma and structured ceremonies. I found what I was looking for in fly fishing.

Fly fishing for me is being outdoors in the cathedral of nature and connected to life. Just being out on the water with a fly rod in my hand puts me in a meditative and contemplative state. There's no room for anger or resentment in fly fishing. If anything, it brings peace of mind and peace to the soul, especially during difficult times. And we all have difficulties in life.

When I was diagnosed with Prostate cancer, fly fishing, and helping others with cancer learn to fly fish as a part of the non-profit group,

Reel Recovery, was just what my spirit needed to help my body fight off the cancer.

~Dave Engen

Fly fishing is one of those things that makes me feel most alive. ~Rick Crawford

Last May I was fishing on a large lake when I noticed a young man and his girlfriend fishing together. It was apparent they were struggling. I watched for a while and then decided to help. To me, a large part of the joy I get from fly fishing is helping others succeed and begin to fall in love with the sport, instead of struggling and giving up.

When I approached them, the young girl immediately asked if I know anything about how to fish this lake and could I help. I helped her rig up with the proper leader length and flies. Somewhat sheepishly, the young man also asked for help. I also shared with them some of the best spots to find fish on the lake.

I watched from a short distance away, and very quickly they were into fish, both of them, and the whoops and hollers of joy were overwhelming. It's important to me to help others fall in love with this great sport, but also make them feel like they accomplished it themselves.

~Greg Keenan

The solution to any problem -- work, love, money, whatever -- is to go fishing, and the worse the problem, the longer the trip should be. ~John Gierach

CHAPTER 22: It Starts and Ends with Heart

Photo courtesy of ©Project Healing Waters Fly Fishing

EPILOGUE

The question isn't who is going to let me; it's who is going to stop me.
~Ayn Rand

EPILOGUE

Neither leadership nor fly fishing are spectator sports. They both involve getting your hands dirty, failing at times, winning sometimes, improving yourself, always.

Don't be afraid to give up the good to go for the great.
~John D. Rockefeller

Leadership is important, now more than ever. As the global population keeps growing, we seem to be assaulting our environment and our social institutions all at the same time, and not with the best of outcomes. It is not my expectation that those who read this book will go forth and become world leaders. But it is my hope that the thoughtful reader will take a few of the lessons and insights contained herein to heart, and then take one or two more steps forward to improve their leadership, and their fly fishing skills.

It's not what you accumulate during your life that matters, it's what you leave behind for the benefit of others. Both leadership and fly fishing provide opportunities to serve others and to build a legacy for future generations. ~Todd Degrosseilliers

To me, the fundamental, most basic lesson gathered from all those I have spoken with and interviewed for this book is that the more you try, and the more you attempt, the better you become. Skills improve with practice. Leadership courage, and confidence improve when you step up and step in.

Fly fishing should not be an escape, but an awakening to the wonders all around us. If you become angry, you are doing something wrong, and it's probably your mindset, not your casting. The same is true for leadership. If leadership feels like a heavy burden and you find yourself getting angry at your staff or the business situation in general, you're doing something wrong. There are far more positives and benefits from being in a position of leadership than negatives. So again, it's probably your mindset. Time for a reboot, and fly fishing is an excellent way to flush out negativity and recalibrate to what leadership is all about.

At least once in your life, you should wade into a fast-flowing river and look upstream. All of the visible landscape — cuts, creeks, draws, hills — is a giant system to deliver water precisely to where you are standing. Waters from multiple sources — springs and small creeks, smaller rivers, distant clouds — are joined right at your feet.

Turn downstream and you suddenly yearn to find out what else will add to this river as it continues on. This fits nearly any aspect of your life: Family, learning, career, politics, and money. Rivers provide the perfect reason to go fly fishing.

~Tom Teague

Each time I travel to the river, my excitement gets the best of me.
I pull into whatever dirt parking area and want to jump out of
the car and yell, "I am here". Usually I step out into the silence
of the natural world. I listen to the river and the wind. I can
almost hear the fish. And I know I am alive. ~Brian Childress

Hopefully in these pages you have learned a few lessons from the skills and beauty of fly fishing and learned something extra about the value of good leadership. To find your way to a great fishing spot you need a good compass. And to find your way as a leader, let fly fishing be your compass.

A Fly Fisherman's Blessing
By John Brady

May the trout rise up to meet you,
as the current runs swiftly by.

May your cast as graceful as an eagle be,
your line drifting freely through the sky.

May quicksilver scales strike your favorite flies
as they dance upon the waters.

May God's limitless bounty fill your heart,
as your spirit becomes one with nature.

CONTRIBUTORS

"Three-fourths of the Earth's surface is water, and one-fourth is land. It is quite clear that the good Lord intended us to spend triple the amount of time fishing as taking care of the lawn."
~Chuck Clark

"It was only on the river that he found both a sense of place and a place of sense."
~Norman Maclean

The global fly fishing community is highly connected, and it's in their ethos and DNA to share ideas, new fly patterns, fishing techniques, innovations, and of course, fish stories. And it's this open spirit of sharing that has made this book possible. Without the stories contributed by guides, lodge owners, and businesspeople around the world, this book wouldn't have broken the surface, let alone seen the light of day. Their stories and examples of leadership lessons learned from fly fishing are the backbone of this book. Hopefully, they will stimulate you to engage in the captivating sport of fly fishing and improve your leadership capability as well.

A huge thank you to all those who contributed, and if you are moved, reach out to them for how to get into, or further along in fly fishing.

AUTHORS:

John R Childress
www.johnrchildress.com
john@johnrchildress.com

Christian Bacasa
www.dupeafish.com
christian@dupeafish.com

PHOTOGRAPHERS:

Christian Bacasa
www.dupeafish.com
@dupeafish on Instagram
christian@dupeafish.com

Jay Beyer Imaging
www.jaybeyer.com

Adrienne Comeau
thefemaleangle@hotmail.com

Marcel Siegle Photography
www.sieglephoto.com

John R Childress
www.johnrchildress.com

Yellowstone Valley Woman Magazine
www.yellowstonevalleywoman.com

Angela Hemingway Charles
hemfly@aol.com

Aaron Smith
@mrwerbs on Instagram

CONTRIBUTORS:

Ali Gentry Flota
Owner, El Pescador Lodge, Belize.
www.elpescador.com ali@elpescador.com

April Vokey
Angling video presenter, podcaster, fly fishing ambassador and author
www.aprilvokey.com

Ben Bangham
UK fly fishing guide.
flyfishingben@gmail.com

Ben Wright
CEO – Velocity Global.
www.velocityglobal.com

Bern Johnson
Exec. Dir., Environmental Law Alliance Worldwide.
www.elaw.org

Bob Mallard
Registered Maine guide, author, blogger, native fish advocate.
www.bobmallard.com

Brad Befus
President, Scientific Anglers.
www.scientificanglers.com

Dr. Brian Childress
bchildr@rocketmail.com

Brian Wetter
VP, IT - Infrastructure and Analytics PacificSource Health Plans
BrianWetter@Hotmail.com

Capt Skip Zinc
Florida fly fishing guide.
www.bocagrandeflyfishingcharters.com

Chris Daughters
Owner, Caddis Fly Shop, Eugene, Ore.
www.caddisflyshop.com

Christine Atkins
Digital Merchandising Manager, Orvis
www.orvis.com

Clement Booth
Board Member, Munich RE AG.
Trustee, Salmon & Trout Conservation
www.salmon-trout.org

Craig Langer
CEO/ Co-Founder at The Flybook Reservation Software
www.theflybook.com

Dan Michels
Owner, Crystal Creek Lodge, Alaska.
www.cyrstalcreeklodge.com

Darrell Pardy
President & CEO at Bristol Seafood, Maine.
Serial Entrepreneur and avid fly angler.
www.bristolseafood.com

Dave Engen
Fly angler and Certified Wine Educator, Park City, Utah

David Cargile
FFI certified casting instructor.
Instructor at the Orvis Saltwater Fishing School in South Carolina.
david.cargile@me.com

David Decker
Owner, Completer Flyfisher Lodge, Montana.
www.completeflyfisher.com

Derek Hutton
General Manager, Bairs Lodge, Andros Island, Bahamas.
www.bairslodge.com

Domenick Swentosky
Fly angler, author and blogger.
www.troutbitten.com

Don C. Puckett
President, Texas Fly Fishers of Houston.
www.texasflyfishers.org

Don Childress
Retired Dentist and Fly Angler, Sandpoint, Idaho

Dusty Sprague
Master Certified Fly Casting Instructor, Florida.
www.dustysprague.com

Faye Nelson
CEO, Casting for Recovery.
www.castingforrecovery.org

Forrest Rogers
Owner, Rock Treads and Crazy Creek Products.
www.rocktreads.com www.crazycreek.com

Fred Owusu
Instructor in Human Resources Management, University of Southern
California
fred.owusu@gmail.com

Gary Forster
Retired orthopedic surgeon and keen fly angler

Gilly Bate
UK Travel Director at Fly Odyssey (www.flyodyssey.com).
Professional guide and casting instructor g.bate@flyodyssey.co.uk

Gordon Sim
CEO, Loop Tackle.
www.looptackle.com

Graham Ellis
CEO, Ocean Harvest Technology.
www.oceanharvesttechnology.com

Greg Keenan
Founder and avid fly-fishing enthusiast, the Fly Fishing Insider Podcast.
www.flyfishinginsiderpodcast.com

Harry Salmgren
Secretary, The Grayling Society Sweden.
www.graylingsociety.net

Heather Hodson
Critical care nurse and avid fly angler, Spokane, WA
northwestflygirl@gmail.com

Jackie Kutzer
Outdoor Designer, Orvis.
www.orvis.com

Jason Shemchuk
Fly angler, blogger, author and artist.
www.wadeoutthere.com

Jen Ripple
Editor-in-Chief, Dun Magazine.
www.dunmagazine.com

Joe Dilschneider
Guide and Owner, Trout Stalkers Fly Shop, Ennis, MT.
www.troutstalkers.com

John Green
Retired UK business owner.
Chairman of the Lower Oykel Proprietors.
Board member of the Kyle of Sutherland District Salmon Fisheries.
Board and trustee of the Kyle of Sutherland Fisheries Trust

John O'Connor
Retired Educator, Eugene, OR

John Smigaj
CEO & Co-founder, Trxstle Products.
www.trxstle.com

Josh Dees
COO Interopion (Healthcare Information Software).
www.interopion.com

Justin Fortier
CEO, FYC Labs, San Diego.
www.fyclabs.com

Larry Marsiello
Investor, Strategic Advisor, Indendent Board Member, and former
Vice-Chairman, CIT Group, New York

Luciano Alba
Owner, Estancia Laguna Verde Lodge, Patagonia.
www.estancialagunaverde.com

Mac Brown
Owner, Mac Brown Fly Fish, North Carolina.
www.macbrownflyfish.com

Margot Page
Author of Little Rivers: Tales of a Woman Angler

Mark George
Fly angler and CEO, Atacama Ventures. San Francisco
www.atacamaventures.com

Mark Thompson
Guide, Big Hole Lodge, MT.
www.bigholelodge.com

Michael Daunt
Author and Partner, Hugh Falkus School of Spey Casting, UK.
www.mikedaunt.com

Michael J McNally
Business consultant and fly angler.
michael@aivia.com

Michael Marx
Fly fishing author, Founder and Senior Strategic Advisor, CorpEthics.
www.corpethics.org

Michaela Merrill
Branch Manager, Bank of the West, Colorado, and Entrepreneur.
www.isotericsapparel.com

Oliver White
Lodge owner (Abaco Lodge and Bair's Lodge, Bahamas) and avid fly angler.
www.oliverwhitefishing.com

Pat Pendergast
Director of International Travel, The Fly Shop.
www.theflyshop.com

Paul Hoobyar
Founder, Watershed Initiatives LLC, Eugene, OR.
www.watersheds.com

Pete Tyjas
Editor, Fly Culture Magazine.
www.flyculturemag.com

Prue Leith, CBE.
Author, Restauranteur and Host of Great British Bake Off.
www.prue-leith.com

Richard Commodore
VP Strategic Relationsips. Effie Worldwide.
www.effie.org

Richard Fieldhouse
Owner, Barbless Flies, UK.
www.barbless-flies.co.uk

Richard Sankey
Chairman, Fisheries Management Scotland and Member of Kyle District Salmon Fishery Board, Scotland

Rick Crawford
President, Emerger Strategies – sustainability strategies for the fly fishing industry.
www.emergerstrategies.com

Rick Porcello
Professional Major League Baseball Pitcher

Roger de Freitas
Active philanthropist, passionate about ecology and practical conservation, Advisor to Environmental Law Foundation.
www.elflaw.org

Scott Pope
Senior Financial Advisor.
www.sutainablewealth.com

Scott Wilday
Owner, LidRig Magnetic Nipper System.
www.lidrig.com

Sean Monahan
Chief Operating Officer, Stone Brewing.
www.stonebrewing.com

Stan Golub
CEO Reel Recovery.
www.reelrecovery.org

Stanislaw Cios, Ph.D.
Polish economist, biologist, diplomat.
Stanislaw.Cios@outlook.com

Tana Hoffman
Owner, Mountainist – outdoor sports and lifestyle rental gear
for women.
www.mountainist.com

Tate Cunningham
Co-founder, Moonshine Rod Company, Tennessee.
www.moonshinerods.com

Todd Aaronson
CEO at Modesto Convention & Visitors Bureau, Inc.
www.visitmodesto.com

Todd Degrosseilliers
CEO, Project Healing Waters Fly Fishing.
www.projecthealingwaters.org

Tom Melton
Fly angler and leadership consultant.
www.meltonleadership.org

Tom Sadler
Deputy Dir. Marine Fish Conservation Network.
www.conservefish.org

Tom Teague
Business Communications Consultant, fly angler and blogger.
www.tomteague.com

Tucker Horne
Chairman & CEO, TH Digital Media Inc. and Team Manager, USA
Youth Fly Fishing Team.
www.thdigitalmedia.com

Victor Lipman

Management Author and Business Speaker, Forbes contributor, President at Howling Wolf Management Training, LLC.

www.howlingwolfmanagement.com

Wade Fellin

Owner, Big Hole Lodge, Montana and chairman of the Big Hole River Foundation.

www.bigholelodge.com

ABOUT THE AUTHORS

JOHN R CHILDRESS

My first lesson in leadership came in 1980 when I helped the leadership team after the Three Mile Island Nuclear Plant disaster. My role as consultant to the CEO and Senior Team was to build a sustainable leadership and safety culture. For the next 38 years TMI was the safest and most productive nuclear plant in the world.

I cofounded the first international leadership and culture consulting firm in 1978 and ran it as CEO and President until 2001, when I retired to do independent advisory, consulting, and write business books. Along the way I have worked on turnarounds for Ford and Lycoming Engines, team alignment for CNH Industrial, Textron, McDonald's, British Gas, Florida Power & Light, and numerous other Fortune 1000 companies.

Growing up on a farm near the Umpqua River in Central Oregon, I learned flyfishing from my father and brothers. Although I consider myself an intermediate fly angler in skill, my appetite for fly fishing is huge, having fished in Kamchatka, numerous Alaska river trips (unguided), Argentina, the Amazon, the Ponoi Peninsula in Russian, Iceland, England and Scotland, Belize, Los Roches, Bahamas, Florida and Africa. I believe important and valuable leadership skills can be learned from flyfishing and I am keen to share these learnings with others thirsty to improve their leadership and fishing skills.

CHRISTIAN BACASA

Throughout life, you gain experience from all sorts of situations. Early in my youth, I was lucky to be mentored by a neighbor Bob Fear, that taught me the value of hard work and thinking through problems with a scientific approach. I instantly applied this to athletics, then translated that to my professional career.

Early in my professional career, I led a sales and service department for Black Diamond Equipment, Ltd., a leading manufacturer of rock climbing and ski mountaineering equipment. Being an avid climber and ski mountaineer myself, I developed many leadership skills as they applied to risk assessment, planning, personal development, and grit. I translated my learnings to the tech industry, where I've been fortunate enough to lead various sales organizations for industry leaders like Oracle corporation and several other leaders in the technology space.

In my mid 30's I was diagnosed with Stage IV Hodgkin's Lymphoma. With various chemotherapies, experimental antibody treatment, radiation treatment, high dosage chemotherapy, and a stem cell transplant, I finally overcame the disease. However, the emotional and physical toll took much more time and effort to recover from than the actual treatments.

During this period, I discovered fly fishing, and shortly after, I co-founded Dupe a Fish, LLC, (www.dupeafish.com) a subscription-based travel booking platform for service providers and anglers in the fishing community. I've since been able to fish in various countries targeting a multitude of species.

WORKS CITED

1. Sean. (2019). Anglers in Chief: US Presidents Who Loved Fishing [Blog]. Retrieved from https://fishingbooker.com/blog/us-presidents-fishing/

2. Farlow, Shannon. What Legendary Journalist Tom Brokaw Has Learned from Fly Fishing. Retrieved from https://www.mensjournal.com/adventure/what-legendary-journalist-tom-brokaw-has-learned-from-fly-fishing/

3. Edwards, Scott. Fly fishing and the Brain. Retrieved from https://neuro.hms.harvard.edu/harvard-mahoney-neuroscience-institute/brain-newsletter/and-brain/fly-fishing-and-brain

4. Henry, B. (2017). Quality of Life and Resilience: Exploring a Fly Fishing Intervention for Breast Cancer Survivors. *Clinical Journal Of Oncology Nursing*, 21(1), E9-E14. doi: 10.1188/17.cjon.e9-e14

5. Conant, D. (2020). Doug Conant: CEOs Must Find Their Courage. Retrieved from https://chiefexecutive.net/doug-conant-ceos-must-find-their-courage/

6. Jaworowski, Ed, (1992) The Cast. Stackpole Books, Harrisburg, PA

7. Oakes, G. (2012). Why slow decision-making is often best – Econsultancy. Retrieved from https://econsultancy.com/why-slow-decision-making-is-often-best/

8. R. Davis, J., & Atkinson, T. (2010). Need Speed? Slow Down. Harvard Business Review Home. Retrieved from https://hbr.org/2010/05/need-speed-slow-down

9. Aalto University (April 28, 2017). Multitasking Overloads the Brain. *NeuroscienceNews*. Retrieved from https://neurosciencenews.com/multitasking-brain-overload-6531/

10. Lipman, V. (2013). An Office Runs Through It: What Fly Fishing Can Teach About Management. Retrieved from https://www.forbes.com/sites/victorlipman/2013/09/18/an-office-runs-through-it-what-fly-fishing-can-teach-about-management/#5dacead7395f

11. Nakamura, J., & Csikszentmihalyi, M. (2009). Flow theory and research. Handbook of positive psychology, 195-206.

12. Pincher, Chapman (31 Oct. 1997) Tight Lines: The Accumulated Lore of a Lifetime's Angling. Robert Hale Ltd, London

13. O'Reilly, Pat. (1997) Match the Hatch. Swan Hill Press

14. Bernhardt, Matthew (Apr 6, 2020) *Is Fly Fishing Dangerous?* Retrieved from https://drifthook.com/blogs/discover/is-fly-fishing-dangerous

15. Perry, Mark. (Oct. 20, 2017) Fortune 500 firms 1955 v. 2017: Only 60 remain, thanks to the creative destruction that fuels economic prosperity. Retrieved from https://www.aei.org/carpe-diem/fortune-500-firms-1955-v-2017-only-12-remain-thanks-to-the-creative-destruction-that-fuels-economic-prosperity/

16. Melton, Tom. (Jun. 29, 2018) 5 lessons for leaders learned from fly fishing in Patagonia. Retrieved from https://meltonleadership.org/5-lessons-for-leaders-learned-from-fly-fishing-in-patagonia/

17. Darling, Marilyn, Charles Parry & Colonel Joseph Moore. (July-Aug. 2005) Learning in the Thick of It. Harvard Business Review

18. https://www.challengergray.com/press/press-releases/2018-year-end-ceo-turnover-report-1452-ceos-left-posts-most-recession

19. Collins, Jim (2009) How the Mighty Fall: And Why Some Companies Never Give In. *Random House Business*

20. Sadler-Smith, E., Akstinaite, V., Robinson, G., & Wray, T. (2016). Hubristic leadership: A review. *Leadership*, 13(5), 525-548. doi: 10.1177/1742715016680666

21. Crown, J., & Coleman, G. (1996). No hands: The rise and fall of the Schwinn bicycle company: An American institution. H. Holt.

22. Santella, Chris. (Apr. 1, 2013) Why I Fly Fish. Stewart, Tabori & Chang

23. Rice, Dan, Karen Kuhla McClone & Lieutenant General Frank Kearney. (August 3, 2020) *Amid Crisis Is The Best Time To Take A 'Tactical Pause'.* Retrieved from https://chiefexecutive.net/amid-crisis-the-time-is-right-to-take-a-tactical-pause/

24. Top 15 Reasons Why Situational Leadership Ensures Business Success, Retrieved from https://www.imd.org/imd-reflections/leadership-reflections/situational-leadership/

25. Fersen, Paul. Fish On: The Tom Rosenbauer Story. Retrieved from https://www.orvis.com/tom-rosenbauer

26. Cahill, L. (2020). Dos and Don'ts For Guided Fishing. Retrieved from https://www.ginkandgasoline.com/fly-fishing-tips-technique/dos-and-donts-for-guided-fishing/

27. Towers Perrin Global Workforce Study. (2007). Retrieved from https://engageforsuccess.org/wp-content/uploads/2015/10/Closing-the-engagement-gap-TowersPerrin.pdf

28. Mirza, B. (2019). Toxic Workplace Cultures Hurt Workers and Company Profits. Retrieved from https://www.shrm.org/resourcesandtools/hr-topics/employee-relations/pages/toxic-workplace-culture-report.aspx

29. Rivera, A. (2019). Netflix's Mission Statement & Vision Statement: A Strategic Analysis - Rancord Society. Retrieved from https://www.rancord.org/netflix-corporate-vision-statement-mission-statement-strategic-analysis

30. Novak, David C. (2012), Taking People with You, Portfolio Publishing

31. Marx, Michael. (2019) Life as a River: Memories & Reflections of a Die-Hard Fly Fisher and Eco-Activist . LiveTrue Books, Imprint of Carroll Communications.

32. Moretti, M. (2018). Learn - 5 Lessons I Learned From My First Full Year of Fly Fishing - The Wade Blog.. Retrieved from https://postflybox.com/blog/2018/11/27/5-lessons-i-learned-from-my-first-full-year-of-fly-fishing/

33. Lawson, T. (2020). The Climate May Be Beyond Your Control, But The Risk Is Not., Retrieved from https://chiefexecutive.net/the-climate-may-be-beyond-your-control-but-the-risk-is-not/

34. Chapin, F. Stuart III, Gary P. Kofinas, and Carl Folke (eds). (2009). *Principles of Ecosystem Stewardship: Resilience-Based Natural Resource Management in a Changing World.* Springer. ISBN 978-0387730325.

35. Nordic-CEOs.com. (July 2, 2020) A Call for a Sustainable Future Society. Retrieved from: https://www.nordic-ceos.com/blog/a-call-for-a-sustainable-future-society

36. McGuane, Thomas. (1999) *The Longest Silence: A Life in Fishing.* Alfred A. Knopf

37. Hunt, V., Yee, L., Prince, S., & Dixon-Fyle, S. (2018). Delivering through diversity. Retrieved from https://www.mckinsey.com/business-functions/organization/our-insights/delivering-through-diversity

38. McKinsey&Co. (May 2020). Diversity Wins: How Inclusion Matters.

39. Morgan, J. (2020). 3 Leadership Lessons From Jeff Dailey, CEO of Farmers Insurance. Retrieved from https://www.linkedin.com/pulse/3-leadership-lessons-from-jeff-dailey-ceo-farmers-insurance-morgan/?trk=eml-email_series_follow_newsletter_01-hero-171-title_link&midToken=AQGJq_IoM4Bv-g&fromEmail=fromEmail&ut=0GpqCIRfveTFk1

40. Hinchliffe, Emma (May 18, 2020). The number of female CEOs in the Fortune 500 hits an all-time record. Retrieved from https://fortune.com/2020/05/18/women-ceos-fortune-500-2020/

41. Zissu, Jared (Oct. 1, 2018) Costa Behind the Guides: Rachel Finn. Retrieved from https://flylordsmag.com/costa-behind-the-guides-rachel-finn/

42. Big Sky Journal. Round Up: 50/50 On The Water. Retrieved from https://bigskyjournal.com/round-up-50-50-on-the-water/

43. Barsh, J., M. Capozzi, M., & Davidson, J. (2008). Leadership and innovation. Retrieved from https://www.mckinsey.com/business-functions/strategy-and-corporate-finance/our-insights/leadership-and-innovation

44. macbrownflyfish.com (Apr.27, 2018) Mop Fly Creator Jim Estes from Bryson City, North Carolina

45. Conway, D. (2020). The leadership advantage hiding in plain sight. Retrieved from https://www.linkedin.com/pulse/leadership-advantage-hiding-plain-sight-dr-jacqueline-conway/?trackingId=doRfKIoRBMA5S%2B54Y9RoFA%3D%3D

46. Lindzon, J. (2014). Why manufacturers spend so much time designing cup holders. Retrieved from https://www.theglobeandmail.com/globe-drive/culture/technology/why-

manufacturers-spend-so-much-time-designing-cup-holders/article21909192/

47. The Lady Magazine (https://lady.co.uk/why-fishing-saved-my-life)

48. Berry, L., Mirabito, A. M., & Baun, W. (2010). What's the hard return on employee wellness programs?. Harvard business review, December, 2012-68.

49. The CIPD. (2019). HEALTH AND WELL-BEING AT WORK [Ebook]. Retrieved from https://www.cipd.co.uk/Images/health-and-well-being-at-work-2019.v1_tcm18-55881.pdf

50. Duhigg, C. (2012). The power of habit: Why we do what we do in life and business. Random House.

51. Ivy Business Journal (Jan-Feb. 2012) Developing Leadershiip Character. Retrieved from https://iveybusinessjournal.com/publication/developing-leadership-character/

52. Schwartzkopff, Norman. (1995) *An excerpt from GEN H. Norman Schwarzkopf's address to the Corps of Cadets at West Point.* Retrieved from https://www.west-point.org/users/usma1995/52324/images/photogallery/4thOfJuly/schwarzkopf.htm

53. Kosur, J., & Marino, J. (2015). The pope, Justin Bieber, and other ridiculous excuses companies have made for poor earnings. Retrieved from https://www.businessinsider.com/excuses-companies-make-for-poor-earnings-2015-10?r=US&IR=T#cisco-blamed-nsa-spying-for-a-decrease-in-hardware-sales-to-foreign-companies-and-governments-10

CPSIA information can be obtained
at www.ICGtesting.com
Printed in the USA
BVHW040311081220
594495BV00002B/4

9 781999 891817